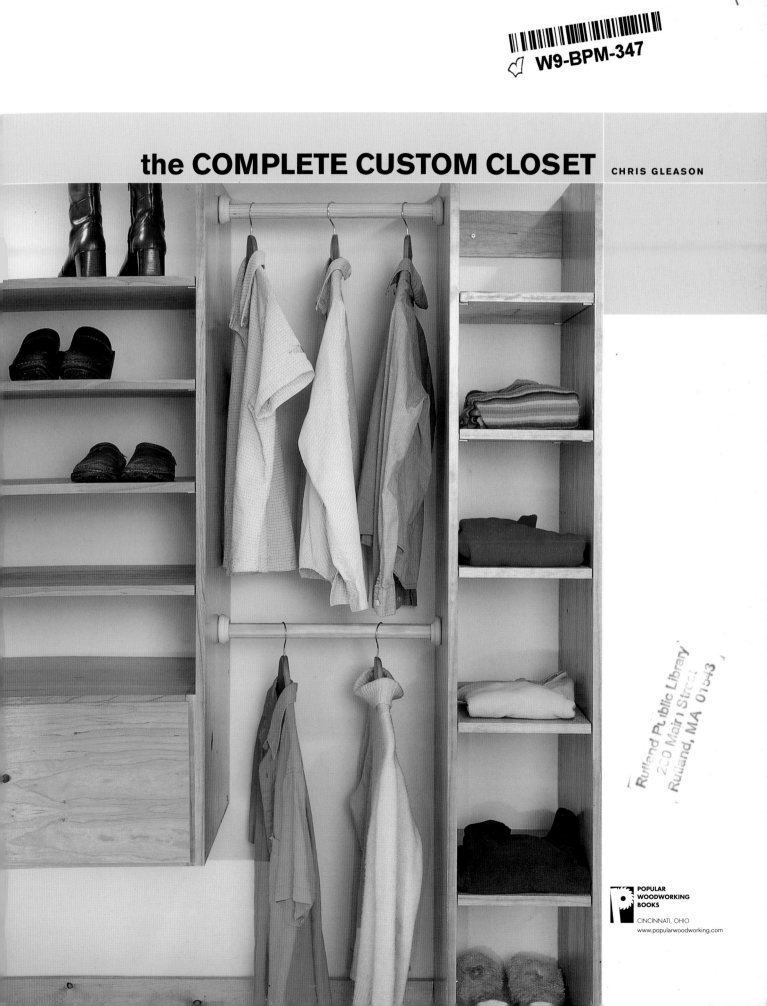

the COMPLETE CUSTOM CLOSET CHRIS GLEASON

POPULAR
WOODWORKING
BOOKS

CINCINNATI, OHIO
www.popularwoodworking.com

READ THIS IMPORTANT SAFETY NOTICE

To prevent accidents, keep safety in mind while you work. Use the safety guards installed on power equipment; they are for your protection. When working on power equipment, keep fingers away from saw blades, wear safety goggles to prevent injuries from flying wood chips and saw-dust, wear headphones to protect your hearing, and consider installing a dust vacuum to reduce the amount of airborne sawdust in your woodshop. Don't wear loose clothing, such as neckties or shirts with loose sleeves, or jewelry, such as rings, necklaces or bracelets, when work-ing on power equipment. Tie back long hair to prevent it from getting caught in your equipment. People who are sensi-tive to certain chemicals should check the chemical content of any product before using it. The authors and editors who compiled this book have tried to make the contents as accurate and correct as possible. Plans, illustrations, photographs and text have been carefully checked. All instructions, plans and projects should be carefully read, studied and understood before beginning construction. Due to the variability of local conditions, construc-tion materials, skill levels, etc., neither the author nor Popular Woodworking Books assumes any responsibility for any accidents, injuries, damages or other losses incurred resulting from the mate-rial presented in this book. Prices listed for supplies and equipment were current at the time of publication and are subject to change. Glass shelving should have all edges polished and must be tempered. Untempered glass shelves may shatter and can cause serious bodily injury. Tem-pered shelves are very strong and if they break will just crumble, minimizing per-sonal injury.

METRIC CONVERSION CHART

to convert	to	multiply by
Inches	Centimeters	2.54
Centimeters	Inches	0.4
Feet	Centimeters	30.5
Centimeters	Feet	0.03
Yards	Meters	0.9
Meters	Yards	1.1

THE COMPLETE CUSTOM CLOSET. COPYRIGHT © 2006 by Chris Gleason. Printed and bound in China. All rights reserved. No part of this book may be reproduced in any form or by any electronic or mechanical means including information storage and retrieval systems without permission in writing from the publisher, except by a reviewer, who may quote brief passages in a re-view. Published by Popular Woodworking Books, an imprint of F+W Publica-tions, Inc., 4700 East Galbraith Road, Cincinnati, Ohio, 45236. First edition.

Distributed in Canada by Fraser Direct
100 Armstrong Avenue
Georgetown, Ontario L7G 5S4
Canada

Distributed in the U.K. and Europe by David & Charles
Brunel House
Newton Abbot
Devon TQ12 4PU
England
Tel: (+44) 1626 323200
Fax: (+44) 1626 323319
E-mail: postmaster@davidandcharles.co.uk

Distributed in Australia by Capricorn Link
P.O. Box 704
Windsor, NSW 2756
Australia

Visit our Web site at www.popularwoodworking.com for information on more resources for woodworkers.

Other fine Popular Woodworking Books are available from your local bookstore or direct from the publisher.

10   09   08   07   06   5   4   3   2   1

Library of Congress Cataloging-in-Publication Data

Gleason, Chris, 1973-
   Closet / by Chris Gleason. -- 1st ed.
      p. cm.
   Includes bibliographical references and index.
   ISBN-13: 978-1-55870-777-1 (alk. paper)
   ISBN-10: 1-55870-777-8 (alk. paper)
   1. Cabinetwork. 2. Clothes closets. I. Title.
   TT197.G487 2006
   684.1'6--dc22
                                    2006015861

Acquisitions editor: Jim Stack
Editor: Amy Hattersley
Designer: Brian Roeth
Production coordinator: Jennifer L. Wagner
Step-by-step photographer: Chris Gleason
Chapter opener photographer: Richer Images
Technical illustrator: Len Churchill

fw
F+W PUBLICATIONS, INC.

ABOUT THE AUTHOR   A self-taught woodworker, Chris Gleason has operated Gleason Woodworking Studio for more than eight years. From his studio in Salt Lake City, Utah, he designs and builds contemporary furniture and cabinetry for a variety of settings. When he's not in the shop, he enjoys mountain biking in the summertime and telemark skiing in the winter. He is also an enthusiastic old-time banjo and fiddle player.

ACKNOWLEDGEMENTS   I'm grateful to Jim Stack and Amy Hattersley at F+W Publications for helping so much to bring this book to life. I'd also like to thank my friends and clients who opened up their homes for the closets you'll see in this book: Their willingness to get involved made for some neat projects. While I'm at it, my wife, Michele, also deserves more than a little acknowledgement for her good nature and patience.

table of contents

introduction

IT SEEMS LIKE EVERYONE I KNOW HAS MORE STUFF THAN THEY DO SPACE TO STORE IT IN. AND for those lucky few who actually have enough space, a lack of proper layout and organization usually lead to limited functionality and diminished aesthetic appeal. Given the vast number of companies that can design and provide stylish closet solutions, it is easy to overcome this hurdle, but not without creating another one: cost. The nicest closet systems, the ones you would happily welcome into your home, generally come with corresponding high price tags. Given the amount of potential usefulness these units offer over their lifetimes, the prices may well be justified, but for those of us who are inclined to do it ourselves, closets represent a great opportunity to save a great deal of money and to add value to our homes.

This book is intended for beginner and intermediate woodworkers who are interested in designing and building custom closets at a reasonable cost. The first part will present some general concepts that aid in planning effective storage. The book is essentially a set of case studies. I began by making a list of the types of closets most people tend to have. Then I chose a real-life example of each and designed an organizer for each one. Each project presents one of these closet types in detail with step-by-step construction photos and a special section to highlight useful techniques or concepts.

Because each individual's lifestyle and storage needs are unique, and because we're usually working with spaces that defy a one-size-fits-all approach, the ideas presented in this book are meant to be modified and improved upon as you see fit. Far from being the final word on the subject, this book is meant to provide design inspiration and practical methods to incorporate as you create the best pos-sible solutions to your own storage needs.

Chris Gleason

Enjoy!

planning for efficient and user-friendly storage

I get a great deal of pleasure from designing good storage systems. Maybe it's just my personality, but the idea of having everything in its place really appeals to me. Beginning the process of organizing can be a daunting task, but this chapter presents a few guidelines to help simplify things.

Keep in mind that closet organizers don't have to be situated inside closet enclosures. It is becoming more and more common to see freestanding closet systems set up in a corner or along the back wall of bedrooms that don't have separate closets and in rooms whose existing closet is too small to be useful. If you have the space, a freestanding closet organizer can be installed just about anywhere.

GENERAL PRINCIPLES

Here are a few general principles I'd like to point out early on. They might sound obvious, but they are fundamental to creating enjoyable and effective storage solutions:

1. BE OPTIMISTIC. As compared to, say, kitchen cabinets, closet systems can be designed to store a lot of stuff while only requiring a modest amount of materials to build. This means you can probably create a great closet organizer on a shoestring budget. If you are willing to spend a little more, your options really open up. This book features a beautiful cherry closet that turned out to be a focal point for the whole room, and the materials cost only a couple hundred dollars.

Because the residential closet design industry has kicked into high gear in the last couple of years, a dizzying array of accessories is now available in home centers or through woodworking suppliers. You might appreciate the convenience and functionality you can acquire by adding a flip-down ironing board or a set of pullout baskets, for example.

2. BE REALISTIC. Most people would like more space to help them get organized, but without moving to a new home or renovating the existing one, that isn't usually a possibility. This just means that you'll have to put some thought into making the most of the space you do have. Even if you don't have room for the walk-in master closet of your dreams, beautiful materials and good design skills can transform even the humblest of projects into jaw-droppers.

3. LOVE IT OR LOSE IT. No organizing process is complete, in my mind, until you've gotten rid of something. The rule of thumb is that if you haven't used or worn something in a year, it needs to go. I'll admit that I don't always maintain this level of ruthless discernment, but the concept is a valuable one. Most storage challenges can be greatly simplified at the outset by paring down the clutter.

tip Whenever I'm planning out storage systems, I try to think ahead to how the user's needs might change in the future. One of the easiest ways to offer some flexibility is by **incorporaing adjustable shelves.** I like to drill rows of $1/4$" (6mm)-diameter holes that can accommodate small metal shelf supports. This approach is simple and inexpensive, and it provides a very quick and easy way to move shelves up or down—or even to remove them entirely. You'll see this concept utilized throughout the book.

STEPS TO A GREAT CLOSET

Although the process of closet design and organization is hardly set in stone, I generally proceed with the following five steps:

1. IDENTIFY YOUR STORAGE NEEDS. What are you trying to organize and store? If, for example, you're trying to organize a bedroom closet, what exactly does that consist of? Shoes? OK, how many pairs? Clothes? All right, let's get specific: Do you have a lot of clothes that need to be stored on hangers, or do you have a lot of bulky items like sweaters that are best stored on shelves or in drawers? This chapter includes specific guidelines to help you allot the right amount of space for the stuff you'll want to store. You may or may not want to perform a precise inventory of your own stuff.

2. EVALUATE YOUR SPACE. What works or doesn't work about your existing situation? Are you faced with a walk-in or a reach-in closet? Do you have adequate space that just needs better organization, or do you need to get really clever to make the most of a small area? How is the lighting? Adding a light fixture can be a huge improvement.

3. REVIEW YOUR OPTIONS. What types of organizers will contain your stuff and provide the most convenience, capacity, accessibility? By taking some time to see what is possible, you improve your ability to design an optimal system for your particular application.

4. WRITE IT DOWN. Getting it on paper will help you to see the potential advantages and disadvantages of various configurations and proportions. It also makes it easier to discuss the project with other people, which is beneficial whether you are collaborating with a client or a domestic partner. When I undertake a project of this nature, I always start by grabbing an empty clipboard or manila file folder. That way, I have a place to store all the paperwork that will invariably pile up—for me, the written elements of the project are just as important as the materials themselves.

I recommend developing two drawings: an overhead view (plan view) and a straight-on view (elevation). I do the plan view drawing first, and it starts with an accurate measurement of the space, which I then draw out. You may want to use graph paper for this.

When I have the design concepts worked out, I prepare materials and cut lists. These lists identify the quantities of materials I'll need to buy, which helps keep my budget on track. They also include a breakdown of the dimensions of the individual components, information which speeds up the construction process tremendously.

5. CONSIDER THE WAY THAT YOU'LL ACCESS THE CLOSET. In some cases, you might not have many options, but sometimes you do, and it can make a world of difference. For instance, sliding doors are usually troublesome because they allow access into only half of the closet at a time, and you can't view the closet's contents at a single glance. In the Laundry Room Closet I removed the sliders and installed a set of standard outward swinging hinged doors. This created a much more appealing and useful space.

In another case, one homeowner decided to remove the wall that blocked most of the front of the closet. For 50 years, the closet had been cramped and difficult to get into, but a few hours of work changed all that and now every bit of the space is organized, accessible, and brightly lit (see Spare Bedroom Closet, page 26).

tip Searching on-line can reveal some great free closet planning resources. In only a few minutes, I discovered two sites that allow users to make really nice drawings of any closet by filling in your dimensions and other parameters. No software downloads are required. A list of useful Web sites is included later in this chapter.

INSTALLATION TIPS

- In general, installations will go more easily if at least one component has some amount of flexibility built into it. Clothes rods and filler panels are perfect examples of this. If need be, floating shelves can be cut down to fit a given space, so they fit this definition as well.
- Set the fixed components in place first (i.e., drawer units, etc.), as the clothes rods can be cut to any length later on.
- I recommend removing cabinet doors and drawers before transporting components to the job site. This helps avoid damage that can occur if moving parts accidentally swing open during transit.
- When placing fixed components inside a closet, you may want to orient them around the door opening for greater accessibility and also better visual appeal. During the planning stages, careful measurement can point out any oddities in the space that you'll have to deal with. In the Kids Closet, for example, the door opening was not located in the center of the closet. I centered the organizer on the door opening for practical and aesthetic reasons, which meant that the clothes rods on the left were about 3" (76mm) longer than those on the right. Since I didn't cut down the clothes rods until the last minute, this wasn't a problem.
- Be ready for creative problem-solving on site. I came up with a nifty solution to the damaged carpeting in the Kids Closet, with minimal time and money required.
- Design with the idea of doing most of the work in the shop, not on site. Whenever I have a choice between doing a particular bit of work in the shop or on site, I always choose to do it in the shop, because it is a more forgiving place to make a mess, and because all of my tools are at hand. Additionally, I find that installations are hectic enough as it is, so I try to simplify them as much as possible, thereby cutting down on potential problems.
- Whenever I have a project that will require an installation, I set it up completely in the shop beforehand. This helps to short-circuit any problems that might come up later, and it allows me to be confident that the installation will proceed reasonably well. It also generally speeds up the installation, because I've already practiced it once.
- Achieving perfectly spaced drawer fronts and cabinet doors before installing the cabinets themselves can be an exercise in frustration. I used to insist on perfection prior to delivery, only to watch in horror as out-of-level floors would cause all sorts of misalignments. Over time, I realized that adjusting doors and drawer fronts on site is very often inevitable, and so I plan accordingly and save myself the time and stress.
- When fastening directly into walls, make sure you use appropriate fasteners and plenty of them. For drywall, I use a lot of toggle bolts when the studs aren't in the right places.
- Sometimes you'll need to remove the baseboards to install a component flush with a wall. I make sure that my installation tool kit includes a pry bar for this reason, as well as a saw to trim the baseboards to fit later on.
- Sometimes you'll run across floors and walls that are a little funky. In such cases, getting your components level and plumb may be less important than making them look right. Be ready to deviate from the rules and use your best judgment in unusual situations.

PRODUCTS THAT MAKE IT EASIER

- Adhesive for melamine
- Self-stick screw head covers—all species and some melamine colors
- Shelf-support drilling templates
- Dowel joinery system
- Pocket hole system
- Cyanoacrylate adhesive with accelerator
- Door and drawer pull installation templates

Clothing Inventory

If you're trying to plan adequate storage for clothing, it can help to add up what you have. You may want to budget in extra space—odds are that you'll buy a new pair of pants now and then. The following chart provides guidelines to help you plan:

Five suits:	12" (30cm) wide, 38" (97cm) long
Five shirts or blouses (on hangers):	10" (25cm) wide, 38" (97cm) long
Shirt (folded):	8" (20cm) wide, 14" (36cm) deep
Sweater (folded):	10" (25cm) wide, 14" (36cm) deep
Pants (folded on hangers):	27" (69cm) long
Pants (on straight hangers):	44" (112cm) long
Skirt:	36" (91cm) long
Dress:	50"–68" (127–173cm) long
Bathrobe:	52" (132cm) long
Suit jacket:	40" (102cm) long
Overcoat:	54" (137cm) long
Shoes:	6"–9" (15–23cm) wide, 10"–12" (25–30cm) long

suppliers of closet accessories

CLOSET VALET
2033 Concourse Drive
St. Louis, MO 63146-4118
866-361-5465
www.closetvalet.com
*Features a safe for protecting
jewelry & valuables*

HANGERCITY.COM
P.O. Box 2384
Riverside, CA 92516
800-600-9817
www.hangercity.com
*A source for closet-specific
organizing accessories*

**KITCHEN ACCESSORIES
UNLIMITED**
1136-1146 Stratford Avenue
Stratford, CT 06615
800-667-8721
www.kitchensource.com
Offers Rev-A-Shelf products

ORGANIZE.COM
P.O. Box 2348
Riverside, CA 92516
800-600-9817
www.organize.com
*Lots of great closet storage
accessories*

**ROCKLER WOODWORKING AND
HARDWARE**
4365 Willow Drive
Medina, MN 55340
800-279-4441
www.rockler.com
*Woodworking tools, accesso-
ries and supplies*

VAN DYKE'S RESTORERS
P.O. Box 278
39771 S.D. Hwy. 34
Woonsocket, SD 57385
800-787-3355
www.vandykes.com
*Hardwood moldings, trim, and
decorative embellishments*

design resources

www.bedbathandbeyond.com
Over-the-door ironing board and tons of other home accessories.

www.closetmaid.com
Has an interactive closet planning utility that poses questions about the closet you're planning: how big it is, its intended use, what you're trying to store, etc. Then it formulates different configurations that might work based on the information you provided. Neat!

www.easyclosets.com
Also features an interactive online closet planner—my favorite one.

www.closetstogo.com
Another interactive closet planner that's worth a look.

www.californiaclosets.com
A very inspiring photo gallery, especially their walk-in closets.

www.closets.com
Another great place to go for inspiration, a lot of attention paid to detail.

www.doityourself.com
Features a large section with very specific information on planning, in particular rules of thumb for space allotment.

www.easytrack.com
An interesting site because they use a wall-mounted track from which to suspend everything, good to see the range of options available.

www.lifeorganizers.com
A series of articles which offer many tips on household organizing.

www.interiordec.about.com
A lot of good info on controlling clutter, etc.

www.diynetwork.com
Features ideas for household organization.

www.realsimple.com
Ideas on organizing, controlling clutter, etc.

www.compoundmiter.com
Great info on trim carpentry, and a link to a must-have book, *Crown Molding and Trim: Install it Like a Pro* by Wayne & Kathy Drake

beyond the basic box

If you'd like to go above and beyond, this is the chapter for you. Rather than present one project in particular, this section is devoted to a survey of the details that can take your closets to the next level. The following chapter, the Walk-In Closet, integrates some of these aspects into a finished closet.

For the moment, though, I hope you enjoy this exploration of the higher end. You may find that you want to incorporate some of these features into your own designs. At the very least, the info here provides some food for thought.

MAKE YOUR CLOSET STAND OUT

There are a few basic factors which can make a closet stand out:

1. MATERIALS. Higher end, carefully finished hardwoods and hardwood veneers, as compared to painted MDF. This extends to using higher quality hardware. The difference between top- and medium-quality drawer slides, for example, is huge.

2. AMOUNT OF ATTENTION PAID TO THE AESTHETICS. There is a world of difference between a purely functional closet and one that has been carefully designed with beauty in mind. This involves questioning every component in the process and deciding how it can be made more attractive and refined. Instead of having open shelves across an entire wall, for example, a couple of doors that conceal the clutter might be more appealing. And instead of using flat panel doors, you might opt for frame and panel doors with a routed edge profile that matches the crown molding. Glass or frosted glass panels can also look great in cabinet doors. There is basically no limit to the way you can beautify a given design, and it often doesn't cost that much more—you just have to think through the details.

Consider, too, architectural trim or any kind of display—a place for an orchid or a vase with fresh flowers—though these things are not at all functional. In addition to being attractive, such touches have symbolic importance—they are acknowledgments of the value of admiring beauty beyond its functional value. A niche with a statue makes a strong statement about the conspicuous transcendence of functionality.

3. SIZE AND SETTING. A small closet can be made to feel luxurious, but a large closet, treated in the same way, will generally feel more luxurious. For one thing, the visual impact is greater, but part of the impact also comes from the fact that when you have more space, you have more opportunities for useful and interesting design details.

A large closet (by which I mean a walk-in) ideally might have a place to sit—how civilized!—and a center island on which you can lay out garments for folding or sorting. Depending on your aesthetics and practical needs, either of these items could be plain or fancy, but having the option would be pretty heavenly, regardless.

In addition to the size of a closet, its overall form is a big consideration. If you have a walk-in closet, the natural light let in through a window, and if you're lucky enough, a pretty view, would be ideal. Sometimes you have no choice about where a closet is located and you have to settle for a spot underneath the stairs, but if possible, full-height ceilings are terrific.

4. GIZMOS & GIMMICKS. Pullout shoe trays might not be necessary but they are exactly the kind of thing which helps to distinguish a high-end closet. Jewelry drawers with hardwood dividers and a velvet lining are another great example of the kind of useful and interesting touches that take a design to the next level. Suggested sources include Rockler, Woodcraft and local home centers.

5. ACCESSIBILITY. In the Spare Bedroom Closet, I actually removed a wall to improve the unfriendly and impractical space layout. The finished result is a focal point for the room. It took about two days to cut out the wall, frame in the new opening and install drywall, but it was the only way to do it right. I could've put in the nice organizer that I designed and made, but it still would've been cramped and uninviting.

Luxuries and Embellishments

Architectural Trim
- fluted columns
- rosettes
- beadboard paneling
- crown molding
- framed artwork
- mirror with a hardwood frame
- complex door styles
- full-length mirror
- wall niche to display a sculpture
- ornate door and window casings
- aromatic cedar lining

Lighting
- can lights
- undercounter lights
- wall sconces
- natural light from a window

Storage Embellishments
- drawer dividers, organizers
- tie racks
- coat hooks
- hidden safe
- laundry hampers
- roll-out shoe shelves
- pullout baskets & bins

Functional Embellishments
- ironing board (flip down or drawer-mounted)
- a seating area (perhaps a window seat)—nice for sitting down to put on shoes
- center island for folding clothes and additional storage

HOW TO MAKE A FRAME AND PANEL CABINET DOOR

Door making can be a rather involved process, but I'll simplify it here—you can always embellish on your own to make your project extra special.

1 Once you have an accurate measurement for the finished door, you can start to make a list of the parts you'll need. A frame and panel door is usually comprised of five parts: a center panel, generally $1/4$" (6mm) thick, and a solid wood frame, which consists of two vertical stiles and two horizontal rails. I usually mill an extra frame part or two because it doesn't take much extra time, and it will be well worth it if you make a mistake later on and need a replacement.

2 Once the lumber has been jointed and planed to a uniform thickness, you can rip a $1/4$" (6mm) wide × 1" (25mm) deep groove on the inside faces of the stiles and rails. To accomplish this, you could use a router table, a dado blade or a regular table-saw blade (which will require making two side-by-side passes). For a small quantity of parts, I usually find this third option to be the quickest since it is easiest to set up. The rails will have a 1"-long (25mm) tenon cut onto each end, and the tenons will be glued into the grooves. You'll need to establish the width of the stiles and rails—in this case, I chose 2" (51mm). In this example, I'll build a door that measures 24" (610mm) tall by 14" (356mm) wide, so that means that we'll need two stiles that are 24" (610mm) in length and two rails that are 12" (305mm) long.

3 To mill a tenon on the ends of the rails, I use a tenoning jig that rides across the surface of the table saw. You can find one new for under $100, and I consider it essential if you plan to build more than a few doors. You could also use a band saw or a table saw and a miter gauge. With the joinery completed, you can cut the panel to size. A plywood panel should fit snugly into the groove, but a solid wood panel will need to have room to expand or contract, so make sure you have a good understanding of seasonal wood movement if you'll be attempting this.

4 Prior to assembly, I recommend making sure the inside faces of the stiles and rails have been sanded smooth. Once the door is assembled it is very difficult to sand these areas.

5 After test-fitting the parts, you can glue up the door. Make sure to wipe any glue squeeze-out from the corners immediately, as glue that has had a chance to set up in the nooks and crannies will be very hard to remove.

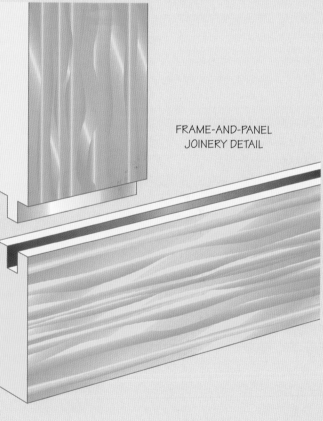

FRAME-AND-PANEL
JOINERY DETAIL

6 You'll need to measure the diagonals to make sure the door is square. The diagonals need to be exact. If they're out of square, I place a clamp across the diagonal that is too large and give it a gentle squeeze. It should slide right into place.

7 Once the glue has cured, you can sand the face of the door frame and its edges. I don't sand the panel once it has been enclosed in the frame, as it is harder to sand evenly. Depending on the overall style and look you're going for, you can rout the outside edges of the door on a router table or with a hand-held router.

8 To add another interesting detail, you can make a small molding on your router table and apply it to the edge of the panel where it meets the stiles and rails.

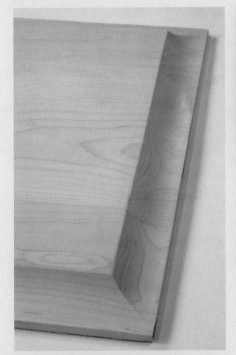

10 A word of caution: These bits must be operated carefully. Don't try to remove too much material at once, and hold the panel very firmly as you make your passes.

9 If you'd like to make a true raised-panel door, the same process applies. Instead of the plywood center panel, though, you'll need to glue up a solid wood panel about ⅝" (16mm) thick. Once it has been squared up and sanded, you can run it across your router table equipped with a panel raising bit.

SAMPLE RAISED-PANEL
DOOR CONSTRUCTION
(SIDE VIEW)

EDGED-PANEL DOORS

If you're using MDF door panels with a painted finish, you can use a hand-held or table-mounted router to create a decorative edge profile. If you're using a veneered plywood, though, a hardwood molding will neatly conceal the plies on the edges of the door panels. The moldings are easy to make with a router table, and your choice of profile will contribute to the style of the finished product. Complex ogee moldings will complement a traditional design, for example, while a simple bullnose may work with a more modern look. If your design calls for the use of contrasting wood species or stains, moldings are a nice way to work that in. I like to make the moldings first, then attach them, although you could attach wooden strips to the door panels first, then rout the profiles.

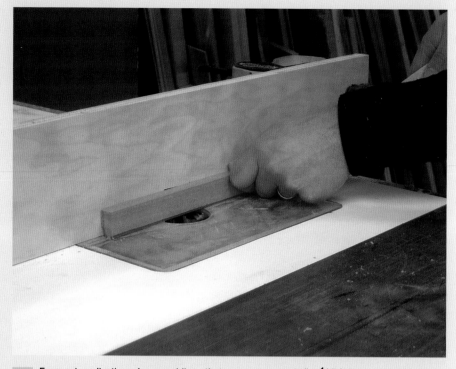

1 For most applications, I use moldings that measure around 1" × ½" (25mm × 13mm), but you may want to experiment with different sizes and see what looks best. I use a sacrificial fence clamped to my router table's fence so that the bit is only partially exposed. This allows me to expose only as much of the bit as I need. I suggest cutting most profiles in several passes. It's safer and usually provides a neater, crisper profile.

2 You could even make the moldings quite large for a faux frame and panel look.

3 I attach the moulding with glue and nails.

4 Miter joints allow the profile to wrap seamlessly around the panels.

5 The result is an attractive door or drawer front.

6 A profile adds to the final result.

MAKING A JEWELRY DRAWER

This refined accessory adds a real touch of luxury to high-end master bedrooms. It's lined with velvet and boasts hardwood dividers. You could add a lock if security is an issue.

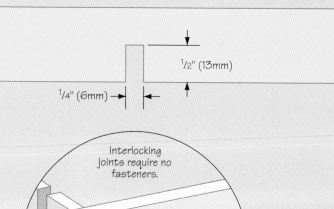

1/2" (13mm)

1/4" (6mm)

Interlocking joints require no fasteners.

1 A jewelry drawer starts out like any regular drawer, built in the usual manner. The velvet bottom is made by wrapping a 1/4"-thick (6mm) piece of plywood with velvet. I use a spray adhesive on the underside of the false bottom to secure the velvet.

2 This false bottom is then dropped into the drawer—note that you must size it 1/8" (3mm) smaller than the drawer's interior.

3 To make the dividers, I start with a 1"-thick (25mm) piece of hardwood lumber. For an 18"-wide (457mm) drawer, I would ideally start with a piece that measures 24" × 6" (610mm × 152mm).

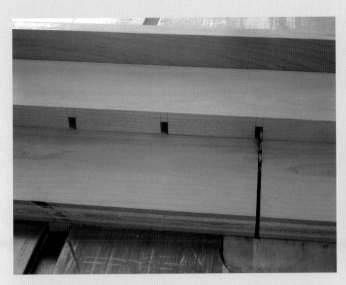

4 Using a miter gauge or a table-saw sled, I cut a series of dados across the piece of wood. The dadoes should be spaced equidistant from one another and should be as wide as the finished dividers will be [about $1/4$" (6mm) wide].

5 The depth of the dadoes should equal half the height of the block of wood. Once the notches are done, you can put a regular blade back on the table saw and rip the block of wood into $1/4$" (6mm) strips.

6 You'll turn half of the strips upside down and keep the other half right-side up.

7 Go ahead and assemble the grid. When you do, it'll become clear which ends you'll need to trim to get the grid to fit into your drawer. This method is handy because you can make a bunch of strips ahead of time and later cut them down to any length that you need. It's also faster and easier to layout this way.

DRAWER CONSTRUCTION

In this book, I've assembled drawers with nails, screws and pocket screws. For high-end projects, when time isn't tight, I sometimes get out my dovetail jig, which is always a satisfying undertaking. As a midrange alternative, I occasionally use rabbet and dado joints in my drawer construction. This provides a clean look with no exposed fasteners. I use my table saw, although a router table and a straight-cutting bit would be effective as well. Here's the process I use:

1 I cut the parts to size on my tablesaw.

2 I cut a dado into each side panel near the ends, where the front and back panels will attach.

3 I trim the front and back panels to create a tongue. A rabbet may be cut into just one side, or both sides could be rabbeted.

4 When done properly, the tongue fits into the dado without force. I lock it into place using wood glue.

DRAWER CONSTRUCTION

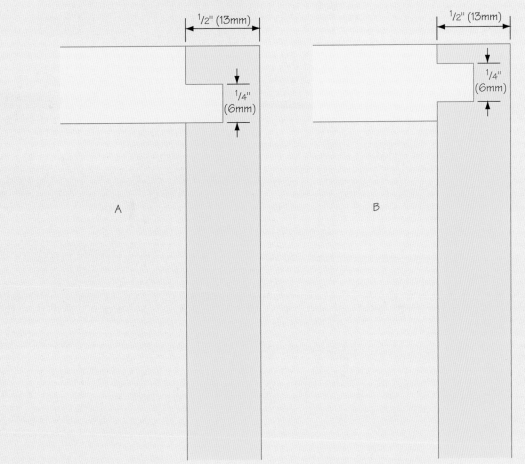

1/2" (13mm)

1/4" (6mm)

A

1/2" (13mm)

1/4" (6mm)

B

spare bedroom closet

This closet has several

functions. Because it is located within a
spare bedroom, it must accommodate the
clothing of occasional out-of-town visitors.
Year round, however, it is also a convenient place to consolidate any overflow that
doesn't fit in the home's other closets. For
this reason it was important that the design
could accommodate a substantial amount of
hanging space. It also serves double-duty,
storing miscellaneous household objects such
as holiday decorations, luggage and other
seldom used items.

Although the overall size of the original
closet was generous, the storage potential
was completely underutilized. Prior to the
remodel, the closet had a narrow doorway on
the left-hand side, which made it possible to
walk in, but because there was no room to
move around, most of the shelves remained
empty or poorly organized.

To provide an attractive contrast with the
white painted walls, we built the closet system out of cherry plywood that has a deep,
rich finish. We also built 24"-deep (61cm)
components to take advantage of the unusu-
ally deep (42" [107]) closet interior.

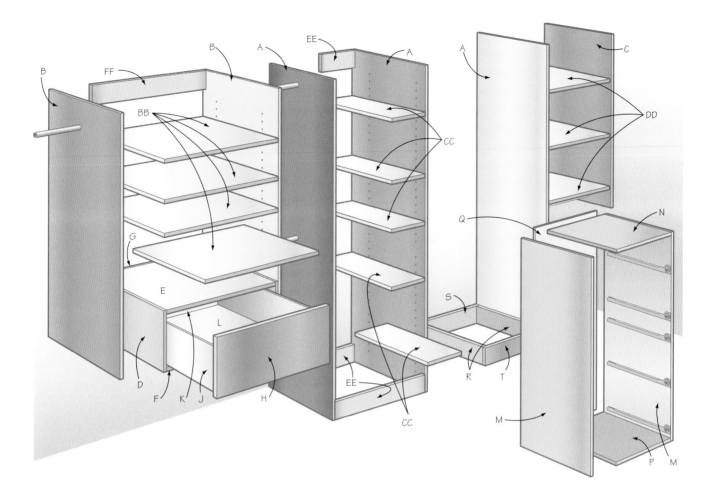

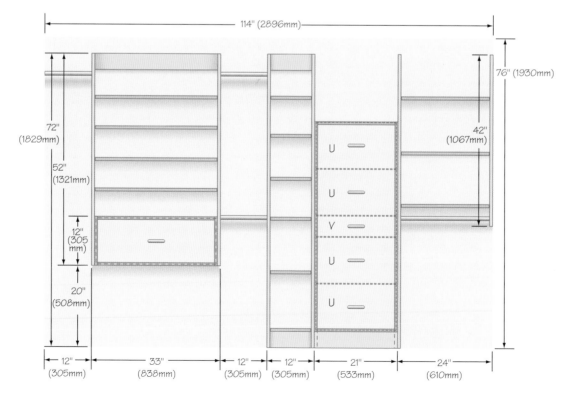

inches (millimeters)

REFERENCE	QUANTITY	PART	STOCK	THICKNESS	(mm)	WIDTH	(mm)	LENGTH	(mm)
A	3	long end panels	cherry plywood	$^3/_4$	(19)	$23^3/_4$	(603)	72	(1829)
B	2	short end panels	cherry plywood	$^3/_4$	(19)	$23^3/_4$	(603)	52	(1321)
C	1	right side wall panel	cherry plywood	$^3/_4$	(19)	$23^3/_4$	(603)	42	(1067)
SINGLE DRAWER BOX									
D	2	sides*	plywood	$^3/_4$	(19)	$23^3/_4$	(603)	12	(305)
E	1	top	cherry plywood	$^3/_4$	(19)	$23^3/_4$	(603)	30	(762)
F	1	bottom*	plywood	$^3/_4$	(19)	$23^3/_4$	(603)	30	(762)
G	1	back*	plywood	$^1/_4$	(6)	12	(305)	$31^1/_2$	(800)
H	1	drawer front	cherry plywood	$^3/_4$	(19)	$11^1/_4$	(286)	$30^3/_4$	(781)
J	2	drawer sides	Baltic Birch plywood	$^1/_2$	(13)	$9^1/_2$	(241)	23	(584)
K	2	drawer front & back	Baltic Birch plywood	$^1/_2$	(13)	$9^1/_2$	(241)	$29^1/_2$	(749)
L	1	drawer bottom	plywood	$^1/_4$	(6)	$22^1/_2$	(572)	30	(762)
FIVE-DRAWER BOX									
M	2	sides*	plywood	$^3/_4$	(19)	$23^3/_4$	(603)	$51^1/_2$	(1308)
N	1	top	cherry plywood	$^3/_4$	(19)	$23^3/_4$	(603)	$19^1/_2$	(495)
P	1	bottom*	plywood	$^3/_4$	(19)	$23^3/_4$	(603)	$19^1/_2$	(495)
Q	1	back*	plywood	$^1/_4$	(6)	21	(533)	$51^1/_2$	(1308)
R	2	base sides*	plywood	$^3/_4$	(19)	4	(102)	$18^1/_2$	(470)
S	1	base back*	plywood	$^3/_4$	(19)	4	(102)	21	(533)
T	1	base front	cherry plywood	$^3/_4$	(19)	4	(102)	21	(533)
U	4	drawer fronts	cherry plywood	$^3/_4$	(19)	$11^1/_4$	(286)	$20^1/_4$	(514)
V	1	drawer front	cherry plywood	$^3/_4$	(19)	5	(127)	$20^1/_4$	(514)
W	8	drawer sides	Baltic Birch plywood	$^1/_2$	(13)	10	(254)	23	(584)
X	8	drawer fronts & backs	Baltic Birch plywood	$^1/_2$	(13)	10	(254)	$17^1/_2$	(445)
Y	5	drawer bottoms	plywood	$^1/_4$	(6)	$22^1/_2$	572)	18	(457)
Z	2	drawer sides	Baltic Birch plywood	$^1/_2$	(13)	4	(102)	23	(584)
AA	2	drawer fronts & backs	Baltic Birch plywood	$^1/_2$	(13)	4	(102)	$17^1/_2$	(445)
MISCELLANEOUS PARTS									
BB	4	floating shelves	cherry plywood	$^3/_4$	(19)	22	(559)	$31^1/_4$	(794)
CC	5	floating shelves	cherry plywood	$^3/_4$	(19)	$23^1/_2$	(597)	$10^1/_4$	(260)
DD	3	floating shelves	cherry plywood	$^3/_4$	(19)	$23^1/_2$	(597)	$22^1/_4$	(565)
EE	3	back wall stretchers	cherry plywood	$^3/_4$	(19)	4	(102)	$10^1/_2$	(267)
FF	1	back wall stretcher	cherry plywood	$^3/_4$	(19)	4	(102)	$31^1/_2$	(800)

*These parts can be made of a less expensive, secondary material because they won't show after installation.

hardware & supplies

6 sets	22" (550mm) long, $^3/_4$" extension Blum undermount drawer slides
6	drawer pulls
3	12" (305mm) hanging rods
1	24" (610mm) hanging rod
4 sets	hanging rod support hardware
48	5mm shelf pegs
	$^7/_8$" (22mm) cherry edge-banding

component listing

Single Drawer Box:	12" high × $31^1/_2$" wide × 24" deep (305mm × 800mm × 610mm)
Shoe Rack Divider:	$31^1/_2$" high × $31^1/_2$" wide × 24" (800mm × 800mm × 610 mm)
Tall Drawer Cabinet:	57" high × $19^1/_2$" wide × 24" deep (1448mm × 495mm × 610mm)

design detail

I'VE RECENTLY STARTED TO ADD AN ELEMENT TO MY DRAWER CONSTRUCTION THAT I THINK CONTRIBUTES A SMALL DEGREE OF REFINEMENT WITH A MINIMAL AMOUNT OF LABOR. INSTEAD OF LEAVING THE TOP EDGES OF THE DRAWERS FLAT, I'VE BEEN ROUNDING THEM OVER WITH A $^1/_4$" (6MM) ROUTER BIT SET INTO MY ROUTER TABLE. I'VE DISCOVERED THAT IT IS CRITICAL TO RIP THE FRONT AND BACK PANELS OF THE DRAWERS $^1/_4$" (6MM) NARROWER THAN THE SIDES—THE DIFFERENCE IN HEIGHT ALLOWS THE ROUNDOVER TO START AND STOP EVENLY. IF THE PARTS WERE THE SAME HEIGHT, THE ROUNDOVER WOULD HAVE AN AWKWARD GAP AT THE CORNERS. SOME PEOPLE MAY NOT NOTICE THIS DETAIL, BUT I CONSIDER IT ESSENTIAL TO BUILDING DRAWERS THAT ARE MORE THAN ORDINARY.

MATERIALS SELECTION

The $^3/_4$" (19mm) cherry plywood has a rich, gorgeous look, but it is not a cheap material to work with. Fortunately, many of the parts involved in building this closet end up hidden from view after final installation. For this reason, I didn't have to shell out the big bucks for premium material, and I even got to use some scrap wood that I'd saved from another project. In the materials list, I denoted the parts that allow for substitution.

In this closet, I used standard issue $^1/_2$"-thick (13mm) birch plywood for the drawers (mostly because I had a lot of scrap to use and I was excited to free up the space in my shop). However, I have recently become a huge fan of pre-finished $^1/_2$"-thick (13mm) plywood drawer stock. You can buy it in 5' × 5' (1524mm × 1524mm) sheets at many lumberyards, and it can quickly be ripped down to whatever dimensions you need for your drawers. The amount of time and effort you save by farming out the finishing is worth the extra cost. For this closet, it might cost you an extra $15 or $20, and

you'll probably save about an hour and a half of tedious work.

I used $^3/_4$" (19mm) rustic-grade cherry for this project. The "rustic" designation means there are small knots in the veneer. If I used A1 cherry grade, I would have paid 30 percent more. For this project, the rustic grade was an ideal material: I stained it rather dark, which minimized the appearance of the knots, and the orientation of the components made the veneer faces less visible.

tip When installing drawer slides, first layout the locations of the drawer fronts. Then install the bottom of the hardware $^1/8$" (3mm) to $^1/4$" (6mm) above the mark indicating the bottom of the drawer front. This will assure ample clearance between the bottom of this drawer front and the top of the drawer front below it.

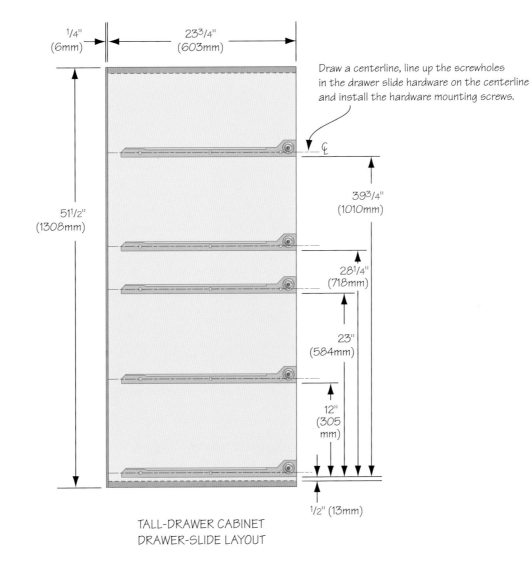

TALL-DRAWER CABINET
DRAWER-SLIDE LAYOUT

1 Cut the end panels first. They are the largest components and the smaller pieces can later be fabricated from their offcuts. Then cut all the other $3/4''$ (19mm) cherry parts.

2 I used $7/8''$ (22mm) cherry edge-banding for all of the exposed edges.

3 When drilling the holes for the shelf pegs, lay out the end panels in matched pairs. (I suggest labeling the back edges of the panels with a marker.) This is easy to do, and failing to do so can wreak havoc later on.

DRAWER BOX HERE

4   I built the base for the tall drawer cabinet from scrap plywood. Only the front piece had to be cherry. The grain orientation didn't matter on the other three sides, either.

5   The tall drawer cabinet is straightforward: It is a four-sided box with the back screwed on.

6   The drawer slides separate into two halves: the cabinet side runner and the drawer rail. In addition, the parts are assigned to either the right of left side of the drawer. The cabinet side runners screw directly onto the inside face of the cabinet sides. To locate the positions of the cabinet side runners, refer to the drawing on page 31.

7 Build the single drawer box and install the cabinet side runners in it. I positioned the front corner of the runners ¹/₂" (13mm) above the cabinet bottom.

8 You can assemble your drawers in any number of ways. I used brad nails and glue. The drawer bottoms fit into a ¹/₄"-deep (6mm) groove that I cut near the bottom of the drawer parts using my table saw.

9 As long as you've positioned the cabinet side runners correctly, the drawers should be a cinch to install. With the drawer placed upside down on a workbench, the drawer rails can be placed on the bottom of the drawer and screwed on. The front edge of the rail should be flush with the front edge of the drawer.

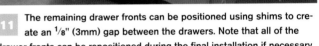

10 These drawer fronts are simple to make, but a bit tricky to attach. Starting with the tall drawer cabinet, you'll need a pair of 4$\frac{1}{2}$" wide (114mm) shims, which will hold the bottom drawer front at the correct height. By removing the second drawer, I had enough space to get a quick clamp in place to hold the drawer front onto the drawer. I secured it from the inside with two 1" (25mm) screws.

11 The remaining drawer fronts can be positioned using shims to create an $\frac{1}{8}$" (3mm) gap between the drawers. Note that all of the drawer fronts can be repositioned during the final installation if necessary.

12 The cabinet top won't allow enough room to get a clamp in place for the top drawer front, so you'll have to pull it out along with the drawer below it. Work carefully and you shouldn't have a problem keeping the parts aligned.

13 For the single drawer box, place a $^1/_2$" (13mm) shim beneath the drawer front to set it at the proper height.

14 The tower is composed of two end panels connected with stretchers. The stretchers are ripped from $^3/_4$" (19mm) cherry plywood and edge-banded on their long edges.

15 Two of the stretchers are positioned at the bottom of the unit, one at the front and one at the back, where they form a base for the bottom shelf. Place the pocket holes for the screws on the back side of the stretchers where they'll be out of sight.

16 The third stretcher is placed at the top of the tower, on the back side. During the installation, you'll screw the tower to the wall through this stretcher.

17 With the right-hand end panel screwed into place, position the drawer unit and make sure it is plumb and level. A few shims will help create a perfect fit. The floating shelves to the right will fit perfectly if you space the end panel $23^{1}/_{4}$" (591mm) from the wall.

18 Screw the drawer unit to the back wall. A stud finder will make it easy to locate the studs.

19 Screw the tower directly to the left side of the drawer unit. It should automatically be plumb, check to make sure it is level. Shim, if necessary, and screw it to studs through its back wall stretchers.

20 The bottom shelf is placed in the tower and secured with construction adhesive.

21 Screw the short end panel into studs in the right-hand wall to create a space for the floating shelves. Place a level on top of the left-hand end panel and across the gap where the shelves will go. When the bubble is perfectly centered, mark the wall accordingly. This indicates the height at which to place the short end panel. Don't simply measure up from the floor—it could be inaccurate due to variations in the height of the flooring.

22 The shoe cubbies above the single drawer unit are made with two short end panels attached to the sides of the drawer box. I ran screws front the inside and the outside the box for maximum holding power.

23 The placement of the single drawer unit is not as critical as it was for the tall drawer unit, because it is surrounded on both sides by clothes rods, which can be cut to whatever length is required. Place this assembly atop a temporary stand and screw the box to the wall, making sure you hit studs. Reinforce the connection to the wall by placing two metal L brackets near the top of the end panels. Secure the brackets to the wall with four toggle bolts. When the whole thing is secure, set the floating shelves inside to create the shoe cubbies.

24 Cut the clothes rods to length, then use a level to determine the correct heights for their mounting brackets. As a finishing touch, I added some crown molding, which is visible in the photo of the finished closet. For tips on installing moldings, see Beyond the Basic Box.

shared master bedroom closet

This project features a generous master bedroom
closet that accommodates the clothing of two adults and a system that keeps its contents orderly.

Because the bedroom itself isn't huge, we decided to install a dresser in the closet so the room could remain more open. The dresser is ideal for small items like socks, underwear and stacks of T-shirts. Above the dresser, we drilled the vertical panels for adjustable shelves. This is a great place for things that don't hang well but can be folded and stacked easily. By positioning the main storage units in the center of the closet, we left enough room on each side for users to easily reach into the edges of the closet alcove. This way, every bit of the space is accessible. The lady of the house owns some long dresses and long coats, but they don't compose the bulk of her wardrobe, so 12" (310mm) of full-height hanging space is enough. The remaining hanging space allows for half-height clothes rods placed one above the other.

The look of the closet takes cues from its surroundings. The maple veneer matches the flooring that runs through most of the house, and the contemporary style fits in nicely with the bright and airy decor. The deep drawers on full-extension glides provide plenty of concealed storage, and the adjustable shelves offer flexibility.

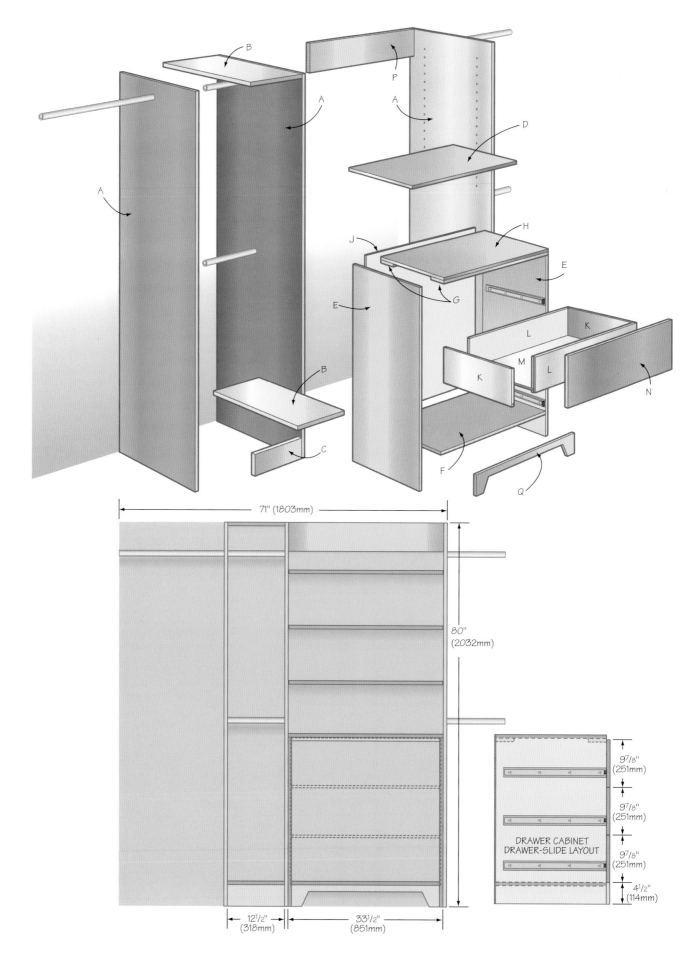

B

A

A

P

A

D

H

J

E

G

E

B

E

C

K

L

K

M

L

N

F

Q

71" (1803mm)

80"
(2032mm)

12¹/₂"
(318mm)

33¹/₂"
(851mm)

9⁷/₈"
(251mm)

9⁷/₈"
(251mm)

DRAWER CABINET
DRAWER-SLIDE LAYOUT

9⁷/₈"
(251mm)

4¹/₂"
(114mm)

inches (millimeters)

REFERENCE	QUANTITY	PART	STOCK	THICKNESS	(mm)	WIDTH	(mm)	LENGTH	(mm)
A	3	vertical partitions	maple ply	3/4	(19)	22	(559)	80	(2032)
B	2	tall hanging unit top & bottom	maple ply	3/4	(19)	22	(559)	12 1/2	(318)
C	1	tall hanging unit toe kick	maple ply	3/4	(19)	4 1/2	(114)	12 1/2	(318)
D	3	adjustable shelves	maple ply	3/4	(19)	21 3/4	(552)	33 1/4	(845)
E	2	dresser sides	maple ply	3/4	(19)	22*	(559)	35 1/4	(895)
F	1	dresser bottom	maple ply	3/4	(19)	22*	(559)	32	(813)
G	2	dresser top slats	maple ply	3/4	(19)	4*	(102)	32	(813)
H	1	dresser top	maple ply	3/4	(19)	22 1/4	(565)	33 1/2	(851)
J	1	dresser back	birch ply	1/4	(6)	35 1/4*	(895)	33 1/2	(851)
K	6	drawer sides	birch ply	1/2	(13)	8 3/4	(222)	19	(483)
L	6	drawer fronts & backs	birch ply	1/2	(13)	8 3/4	(222)	30	(762)
M	3	drawer bottoms	birch ply	1/4	(6)	18 1/2	(470)	30 1/2	(775)
N	3	drawer false fronts	maple ply	3/4	(19)	9 7/8	(251)	32 1/2	(826)
P	1	stretcher	maple ply	3/4	(19)	6	(152)	33 1/2	(851)
Q	2	toe kicks	maple ply	3/4	(19)	2	(51)	30	(762)
R	1	clothes hanging bars	dowel	1 1/4	(32)			13	(330)
S	4	tall hanging unit hanging bar	dowel	1 1/4	(32)			12 1/4	(311)

*Grain orientation doesn't matter on these parts, as they don't show after installation.

hardware & supplies

3 sets	20" (500mm) side-mount slides
3	drawer pulls
5 sets	clothes rod hangers

1 Begin by cutting the three vertical partitions—they're identical, so I cut them all at once, which saved some time and most importantly, ensured that they were consistent.

2 I like to mount shelves on L-shaped supports that fit into $\frac{1}{4}$"-diameter (6mm) holes because they're easy to install and adjust. Drill the necessary rows of holes using a scrap of pegboard cut to the required length. To drill each set of holes consistently, mark the top edge of the pegboard with a highly visible marker. To avoid drilling holes in the wrong locations, use masking tape to cover up the unneeded holes. If I don't have any pegboard around, I just grab a scrap of $\frac{1}{4}$"-thick (6mm) plywood and custom-make a piece to fit the project. In this project, the shelves fit between the two vertical partitions in the right-hand side of the closet. Mark the partitions accordingly, so you can easily sort out and position them in the heat of the moment. In my experience, I have found that anytime you have more than one of something, you have an opportunity to grab the wrong one, so I am obsessive about labeling components. I usually try to put marks in places that won't show after the final assembly—along the top and back edges of the partitions, for example. In this case, I label them partitions 1,2 and 3, from left to right respectively. Partitions 2 and 3 need peg holes from the top down, as shown in the photos. They are not interchangeable, but are in fact mirror images of each other, so be sure to align them as such when you drill the holes. I begin drilling holes 8" (203mm) from the top of the panel and continue until the lowest hole is 44" (1118mm) from the bottom of the panel. The holes are spaced 2" (51mm) apart.

3 The tall hanging unit is constructed as a stand-alone component and lends a lot of strength and stability to the adjustable shelf area to its right and to the clothes rods on its left. It also makes the installation simpler because it is preassembled. The unit is basically built like a bookcase: It consists of two vertical partitions that are held together by a bottom and a top. The bottom and top are glued and screwed to the sides, and the screw heads are covered with wood filler. I created a toe kick area by raising the bottom $4^{1}/_{2}$" (114mm) from the floor, the amount of space that corresponds with the height of the dresser's toe kick.

4 The $^{1}/_{4}$" (6mm) plywood back is attached with screws and glue.

5 The dresser is essentially a four-sided box, with the back glued and nailed on. A separate top cap will finish it off and hide the exposed plywood edges which would otherwise be visible from above. Begin the dresser by cutting the sides and bottom to size. The bottom is glued and screwed into place; the sides overlap it. You'll notice that I inset the bottom $4^{1}/_{2}$" (114mm) from the bottom edge of the sides. The toe kick will be installed in this space.

6 The two top slats are attached in the same manner as the bottom, except they are positioned flush with the top of the cabinet sides.

7 Cut out the back and nail it in place.

8 For the toe kick, cut out a rectangle that will fit precisely into the recess at the bottom of the cabinet. I decided to add a decorative cut to create some visual appeal.

9 The toe kick is screwed and glued into place.

10 You'll cover all exposed plywood edges with iron-on edge-banding. The installation takes some time to get the hang of, but goes quickly once you're up to speed. You can wait until all of the parts are cut out and ready to edge-band so you can do them all at once, or you can do them a few at a time as you feel like it. It is marginally quicker to do them all at once, but sometimes my attention span just can't handle that, so I break it up a bit and find that it goes very quickly. To each his own, in this regard.

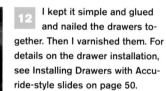 The cabinet has three drawers which are all uniform in size, saving you a bit of time during the design and construction phases because all of the parts will be identical. You'll need to cut $1/2$" (13mm) plywood to the dimensions indicated on the cut list. Then you'll rip a $1/4$" (6mm) groove into the drawer stock $1/2$" (13mm) above the bottom edge of the sides. You can use a router table, a dado blade on the table saw, or a standard table saw blade. Move the fence $1/8$" (3mm) and make a second pass. Whatever you use, make sure the groove is sized appropriately for the drawer bottom.

I kept it simple and glued and nailed the drawers together. Then I varnished them. For details on the drawer installation, see Installing Drawers with Accuride-style slides on page 50.

13 The plan called for three adjustable shelves, which are simple rectangles. The opening measures 33$\frac{1}{2}$" (851mm) wide, so I subtract $\frac{1}{4}$" (6mm) from this dimension to get the width of the shelves [33$\frac{1}{4}$" (851mm)]. Adjustable shelves need a little wiggle room [about $\frac{1}{8}$" (3mm) on each side] so they can move in and out easily without causing any damage to the vertical partitions. We also needed a 33$\frac{1}{2}$"-long (851mm) stretcher between vertical partitions 2 and 3. It will be positioned at the top rear corner of the partitions and screwed directly into a stud on the back wall.

14 By setting up the components in the shop beforehand, I can rest assured the installation will go smoothly. Because this design is pretty simple, I'll just have to screw the components to the wall and install the clothes rods.

installing drawers with Accuride-style slides

TO BEGIN WITH, YOU NEED TO MAKE SURE THAT THE DRAWERS ARE SIZED PROPERLY. ACCURIDE-STYLE SLIDES ARE $\frac{1}{2}$" (13MM) WIDE (A SET OF TWO WILL TAKE UP 1" [25MM] WITHIN THE CABINET), SO TAKE THAT INTO ACCOUNT. IF THE INTERIOR WIDTH OF YOUR CABINET IS $22\frac{1}{2}$" (572MM), THEN THE OUTSIDE WIDTH OF THE DRAWERS NEEDS TO BE $21\frac{1}{2}$" (546MM). WHEN IN DOUBT, IT IS BETTER TO BE $\frac{1}{16}$" (2MM) OR EVEN $\frac{1}{8}$" (3MM) TOO NARROW RATHER THAN TOO WIDE: YOU CAN ALWAYS USE SHIMS TO TAKE UP THE SLACK, BUT A DRAWER THAT IS TOO LARGE WILL HAVE TO BE CUT DOWN AND REBUILT.

1 The process is pretty simple: First install the sliders into the cabinet, then attach the drawers to the sliders. I start by placing the cabinet on its side, which is easier than fighting against gravity. Position the sliders more or less in the center of the spot where the drawers will fall, and rip some scrap stock into spacers to ensure consistent placements. The front edge of the drawer slide lines up exactly with the front edge of the cabinet sides. It may help to extend the line onto the front edge of the side so that you can see that you're centering the slide properly.

2 Affix each slide with three screws, then flip the cabinet over and repeat the process on the opposite side. With the dresser in an upright position, set $\frac{3}{4}$"-thick (19mm) spacers on the cabinet bottom (note that I colored the spacer green in the photo so it would stand out). The bottom drawer can then slide into the cabinet most of the way—let it protrude about 2" (51mm) or so, and it will be level with the bottom of the dresser. Extend the sides so their front edges are flush with the front of the drawer.

3 Place a screw into the first hole on each side of the drawer, then pull the drawer out. Apply downward pressure on the drawer to make sure it is sitting flat and level, then screw in the back of the slides as well. When the bottom drawer is in, remove the spacers and place them on top of the drawer—this paves the way for the next drawer to be installed. The top drawer is installed in the same way.

4 A few tricks of the trade will take some of the frustration out of hanging drawer fronts. Starting with the bottom drawer, put the drawer front into position, then squeeze it tightly against the drawer box. Working slowly and carefully, pull the drawer out a few inches and use a quick-clamp to hold the drawer front in place. Making sure not to jostle the drawer front, work in a couple of screws from the inside of the drawer. With the drawer closed, set a pair of shims on top of the drawer front and place the next drawer front on top of them—this will create the desired 1/8" (3mm) gap between the drawer fronts.

5 I repeat this process all the way up the cabinet. If a drawer front ends up crooked, just remove the screws and adjust it so that it lines up correctly. Experience has taught me to install a cabinet on site before I try to get the drawer fits exactly right: More than once, I've lined up drawers perfectly in the shop, then delivered them to an out-of-level site and watched in horror as my precise fits went askew. To line up the drawer pulls, I suggest purchasing an inexpensive plastic template, available at most home improvement stores. They feature hole spacing for the most commonly sized pulls and knobs.

closet-based
home office

Converting a closet into a mini home office is an

option for those who don't have an entire room to sacrifice. In this example, the closet is left open because I think it looks great, and I keep it tidy enough to be on display most of the time. If you work amidst clutter, though, you can easily add a set of doors.

The most important part of planning this closet is evaluating your storage needs and working style. I already owned a simple wooden stool that is comfortable for me to sit at, so I played around with a few measurements and decided on a desktop height of 38" (965mm). I also knew that I wanted as big of a desktop as possible because I need to spread out as I work. This requirement basically divided the space into upper and lower portions. I realized that I could work more storage into the lower area, so I kept the upper area pretty minimal. I like having open shelves to show off knickknacks, and I can always incorporate baskets and bins later on if I need to.

I had a lot of stuff to squeeze into the lower area. One of the drawers is very shallow and functions as a roll-out printer tray, which frees up a lot of desktop space and eliminates some visual clutter. I also have a pullout recycling bin, and five deep drawers that hold everything from envelopes to files. For file storage, I used aftermarket drop-in file rails that I bought at an office store. I left one cabinet mostly open so that it could hold a computer tower should I ever give up my trusty laptop. I also dedicated a small portion of that same cabinet to hold cables and cords.

I used ¾" (19mm) MDF because it speeds up the construction process (you don't need to do any edge-banding). It is also good for the budget. The expense in this project lies in the drawer slides and the recycling pullout rather than high-end veneered plywoods. MDF also takes paint beautifully, which allowed me to experiment with some nifty color combinations. This particular arrangement of doors and drawer fronts really asks for a playful use of color.

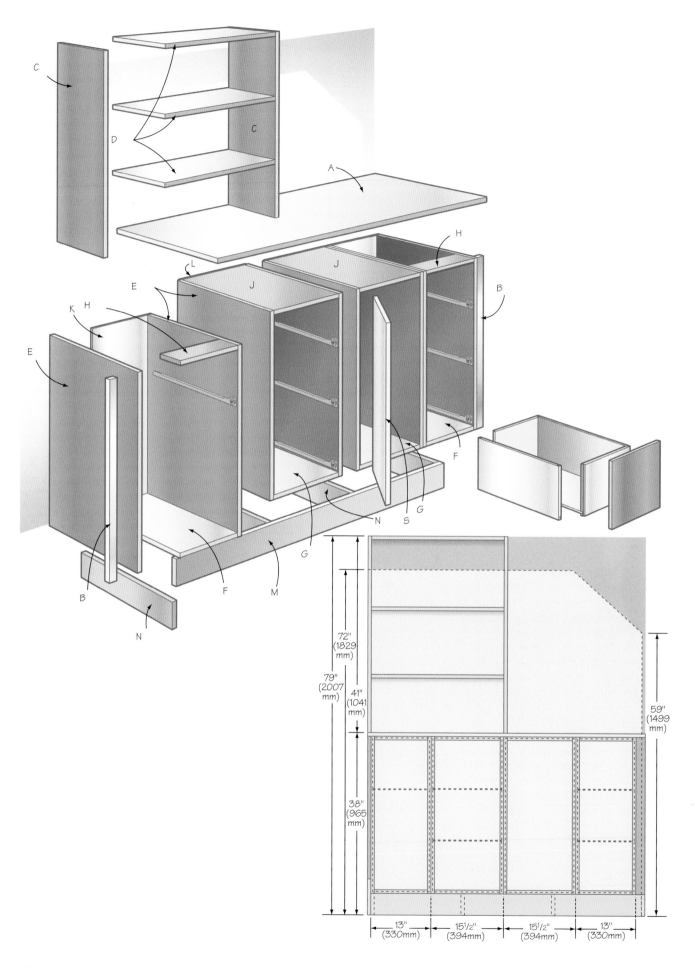

inches (millimeters)

REFERENCE	QUANTITY	PART	STOCK	THICKNESS	(mm)	WIDTH	(mm)	LENGTH	(mm)
A	1	desktop	MDF	3/4	(19)	27 1/2	(699)	61	(1549)
B	2	filler strips	hardwood	3/4	(19)	1 1/2	(38)	36	(914)
C	2	bookcase sides	MDF	3/4	(19)	12	(305)	41	(1041)
D	3	bookcase shelves	MDF	3/4	(19)	12	(305)	28 1/2	(724)
E	8	cabinet sides for A, B, C, D	MDF	3/4	(19)	23 3/4	(603)	32 3/4	(832)
F	2	cabinet bottoms for A, D	MDF	3/4	(19)	23 3/4	(603)	11 1/2	(292)
G	2	cabinet bottoms for B, C	MDF	3/4	(19)	23 3/4	(603)	14	(356)
H	2	upper stretchers for A, D	MDF	3/4	(19)	3	(76)	11 1/2	(292)
J	2	upper stretchers for B, C	MDF	3/4	(19)	23 3/4	(603)	14 1/2	(368)
K	2	cabinet backs for A, D	MDF	1/4	(6)	13	(330)	32 3/4	(832)
L	2	cabinet backs for B, C	MDF	1/4	(6)	14 1/2	(368)	32 3/4	(832)
M	2	cabinet base front & back	MDF	3/4	(19)	4 1/2	(114)	59	(1499)
N	4	cabinet base sides & center supports	MDF	3/4	(19)	4 1/2	(114)	19 1/2	(495)
P	4	drawer fronts for A, D	MDF	3/4	(19)	12 1/4	(311)	10 5/8	(270)
Q	1	door for A	MDF	3/4	(19)	12 1/4	(311)	21 1/4	(540)
R	3	drawer fronts for B	MDF	3/4	(19)	14 3/4	(375)	10 5/8	(270)
S	1	door for C	MDF	3/4	(19)	14 3/4	(375)	32	(813)
T	12	drawer sides	birch ply	1/2	(13)	8	(203)	19 3/4	(502)
U	8	drawer fronts & backs	birch ply	1/2	(13)	8	(203)	9 1/2	(241)
V	4	drawer fronts & backs	birch ply	1/2	(13)	8	(203)	12	(305)
W	2	drawer sides	birch ply	1/2	(13)	2 1/2	(64)	19 3/4	(502)
X	2	drawer front & back	birch ply	1/2	(13)	2 1/2	(64)	12	(305)
Y	3	drawer bottoms	birch ply	1/4	(6)	12 1/2	(318)	19 1/4	(489)
Z	4	drawer bottoms	birch ply	1/4	(6)	10	(254)	19 1/4	(489)

hardware & supplies

trash/recycling pullout: Rev-A-Shelf single bin 35 quart pullout

(#32549 @ Rockler) or similar—minimum opening is 10 3/4" (273mm) wide.

brushed nickel grommet for the desktop

7 sets   20" (500mm) side-mount drawer slides

9   door pulls

component listing

Bookcase	41" high × 30" wide × 12" deep (104 × 76 × 30cm)
Cabinet A	32 3/4" high × 13" wide × 24 1/4" × deep (83 × 33 × 62cm)
Cabinet B	32 3/4" high × 15 1/2" wide × 24 1/4" × deep (83 × 39 × 62cm)
Cabinet C	32 3/4" high × 15 1/2" wide × 24 1/4" × deep (83 × 39 × 62cm)
Cabinet D	32 3/4" high × 13" wide × 24 1/4" × deep (83 × 39 × 62cm)
Desktop	61" × 27" × 3/4" thick (155 × 69 x 19cm)
Base	59" × 21" × 4 1/2" high (150 × 53 × 11cm)

DRAWER LISTING:

Cabinet A:	1 @ 10 1/2" wide × 23" deep × 8" high (27 × 58 × 20cm)
Cabinet B:	2 @ 13" wide × 23" deep x 8" high (33 × 58 × 20cm)
	1 @ 13" wide × 23" deep × 2 1/2" high (printer pullout, top drawer) (33 × 58 × 6.5cm)
Cabinet C:	None
Cabinet D:	3 @ 10 1/2" wide × 23" deep × 8" high (27 × 58 × 20cm)

DOOR & DRAWER FRONTS (ALL FROM 3/4" MDF):

Cabinet A:	1 @ 10 5/8" high × 12 1/4" wide (27 × 31cm)
	1 @ 21 1/4" high × 12 1/4" wide (54 × 31cm)
Cabinet B:	3 @ 10 5/8" high × 14 3/4" wide (27 × 37cm)
Cabinet C:	1 @ 32" high × 14 3/4" wide (81 × 37cm)
Cabinet D:	3 @ 10 5/8" high × 12 1/4" wide (27 × 31cm)

1 Cut all of the parts for the cabinets and their doors at the same time. I recommend labeling the parts, since you'll have quite a stack, and it helps to be organized.

2 The cabinet boxes sit on a single base. It measures $4^1/2$" (114mm) high and spans almost the entire footprint of the niche. I set the sides in about 1" (25mm), just in case the front and back of the base needs to be trimmed for a precise fit. Position the center supports evenly across the interior of the base.

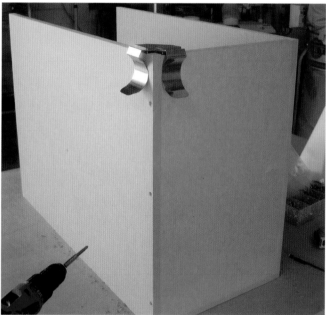

3 To build the bookcase, I used countersunk screws because they're easy to fill and paint over, although you could also use pocket screws, but biscuits, or dados and glue. Rather than place the bottom shelf directly at the bottom of the bookcase, where it would break up the desktop surface, I raised it up 15" (381mm). I didn't need to build a back because this bookcase will be screwed directly to the wall through its left-hand side. Eliminating the back saves time and materials, and it also allows the wall color to show through, which is an important design element in this case.

4 Cabinets A,B,C and D all go together the same way. I used through screws, since the sides won't show and there's no need to conceal the joinery. Just be sure to predrill and countersink for the screws. I also recommend setting the screws a few inches in from the corners if you use MDF, since it tends to split if screws are driven into its edges near a corner. And don't be stingy with the glue—the adhesives will provide a lot of the strength in this case.

5 Since this project allows for some "quick and dirty" construction techniques, you can simply screw and glue the backs directly onto the cabinet boxes.

6 To make sure all the components will go together properly, I always set them up in the shop.

7 The cut list indicates the parts you'll need for the drawers. For specific tips on building and installing drawers, see the Shared Master Bedroom Closet project.

8 Making the doors and drawer fronts for this project couldn't be simpler. No edge-banding is required, and all you need to do is cut out MDF rectangles. To help develop the color scheme for this project, I laid out the doors and drawer fronts in their actual configuration. For me this was much easier and more direct than trying to work on paper.

9 For details on how to install and adjust 35mm Euro-style door hinges, see the sidebar on page 60 and 61.

INSTALLATION

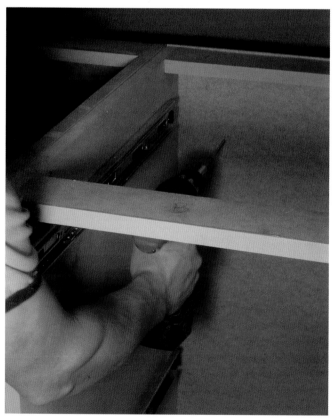

10 Once you've set the base into position and leveled it with shims as needed, you can set the cabinets on it. I pushed the cabinets up against the right-hand wall, then screwed them together. You'll notice that I used a quick-clamp to keep their front edges flush. This configuration left an uneven gap along the left-hand side due to some bulges in the plaster on the wall. I scribed a filler strip to fit this space.

11 I screwed the cabinets into studs in the back wall.

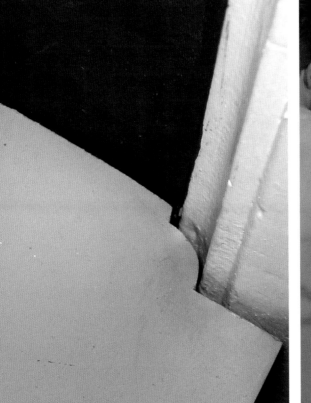

12 In a perfect world, the closet niche would be a precise rectangle, and you could just measure it and cut a rectangle to fit for the desktop. If you're lucky and this is the case, go for it! Otherwise, I suggest using a method for creating a template that will help you to fit a desktop or work surface into an uneven spot. (This also works great for counter-tops, by the way.) See the sidebar on page 62.

13 Set the bookcase directly on top of the desktop and screw it to the wall through its left-hand side.

14 For ease of cable management, I drilled a 2$\frac{1}{2}$"-diameter (64mm) hole through the desktop near its back edge. I trimmed out the hole with a brushed nickel grommet.

tip When it's time to paint, be aware that the cut edge of an MDF panel is a lot more porous than its surface and will soak up more paint. You may need to sand aggressively between coats (use 100-grit paper) to achieve a nice uniform edges.

using 35mm Eurohinges

LOTS OF PEOPLE SWEAR BY 35MM (EUROPEAN-STYLE) HINGES. THEY INSTALL QUICKLY AND ARE EASY TO ADJUST. THEY ARE ALSO AVAILABLE FOR EVERY IMAGINABLE CONFIGURATION: ANGLED CABINETS, BIFOLD DOORS, YOU NAME IT.

1 The hinges come in two parts: the hinge cup and the mounting plate. Start by drilling a hole in the door to hold the hinge cup. You'll need a 35mm or 1³/₈" Forstner bit. To locate the center of the hole for the hinge cup, make a pencil mark ⁷/₈" (22mm) from the edge of the door.

2 Be sure to place the marks far enough from the top and bottom of the door so that the hinges will close without hitting the top and bottom of the cabinet itself—3" (76mm) should do it. For doors longer than 36" (914mm), I recommend three or more hinges. You can secure the hinge cup with two ⁵/₈" (16mm) self-tapping screws.

3 With the mounting plate clicked onto the hinge cup, position the door at its correct height for mounting. I leave a $1/8$" (3mm) gap between the door and front of the cabinet (I just eyeball it, but you could tape a spacer to the edge of the door and then press it tightly into place). Using a pen, or fine marker, mark the locations of the mounting plate holes on the inside of the cabinet. A few screws will secure the door.

4 With the door closed, you can evaluate how it looks. You're checking for three things: When viewed straight on, it should be plumb, and set at the proper height. When viewed from the side, it should be hanging straight: The gap between the door and the cabinet side should be minimal and it should be nice and even with no excessive widening at either the top of bottom. All adjustments are made by turning the screws on the arm of the hinge: You can adjust each hinge from side to side, up and down, and front to back. If you take the time to get a feel for it, this becomes an intuitive process, and you'll just know which screw needs to be turned (and in which direction) to correct an imprecise door fit.

5 Some door arrangements can be pretty complicated, especially when you have a number of doors all lined up next to each other, but you'll prevail by working slowly and systematically, assuming your doors and cabinets are square. I suggest making only one adjustment at a time, then closing the door to evaluate the overall look. Also, I recommend that you wait until the cabinets have been installed before you put any time into achieving perfectly fitting doors. Cabinets tend to sit differently before and after they've been properly leveled and fastened to walls, and this will affect the way the doors hang.

making a desktop template

MAKING A DESKTOP THAT IS BORDERED ON THREE SIDES BY WALLS CAN BE TRICKY, ESPECIALLY SINCE YOU ARE OFTEN NOT DEALING WITH PERFECTLY SQUARE AND EVEN WALLS. FORTUNATELY MY FRIEND DAVE SHOWED ME A NEAT WAY OF MAKING A TEMPLATE THAT YOU CAN TRACE ONTO YOUR DESKTOP BLANK.

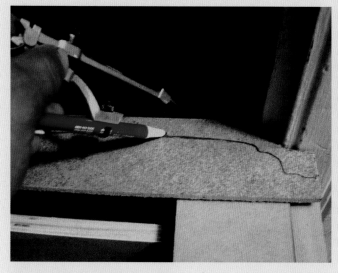

1 To form the template, I use scraps of $1/4$"-thick (6mm) hardboard (masonite) or veneered plywood, ripped into 2" (51mm) widths. Cut one strip for each side that you'll need to scribe and a strip for the front edge.

2 Start with the back edge. Place the strip against the back wall and see how it looks: If there is no space between the strip and the wall, that will save you some time. If there is a gap, however, you'll need to scribe the strip. Set the compass points about $1/4$" (6mm) wider than the gap at its widest point. You can then run the compass along the wall and cut along the line with a jigsaw.

3 The strip should now fit against the wall; a little sandpaper will take care of any anomalies. The left and right sides are done in the same way. Once the strips fit against all three walls, you can connect them at the corners with $1/2$"-long (13mm) screws. The front strip can be secured in the same way. If you take your time with the scribing and cutting, your finished desktop should drop right into place.

scribing a filler strip to a wall

WITH THE CABINETS SECURED INTO PLACE, PLACE THE FILLER STRIP AGAINST THE

WALL AND HOLD IT SECURELY.

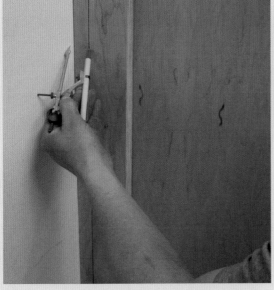

1 Set the compass points about 1" (25mm) apart and move the compass from top to bottom to create a pencil line that mirrors the eccentricities of the wall.

2 With a jigsaw, cut carefully to the line.

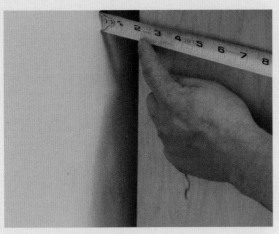

3 To fit the filler to the gap, measure the gap at the top and bottom of the cabinet. In this case, it was about 1¹⁄₂" (38mm) at the top and 1" (25mm) at the bottom.

4 I marked the filler strip accordingly [1¹⁄₂" (38mm) from the scribed line on the top and 1" (25mm) at the bottom], and drew a straight line to connect the two marks.

sports closet

This project is a neat variation

of a walk-in closet—one that isn't used to store clothes. Instead, this area has been designed to give an active family optimal storage space for their sports equipment. They do a lot of cycling in the summer and skiing in the winter, and between the two activities, they own quite a bit of gear. Fortunately, they had a small unused room that we could easily convert to a walk-in sports closet.

After an initial consultation and site measurement, we determined that they would need a wall-mounted ski rack to holds six pairs of skis and also a work area where they could wax skis—the long L-shape countertop provides ample space for this. They also have many pairs of ski boots, which are best stored on open shelves so air can circulate, allowing the boots to dry out between days on the slopes. Small items—such as hats and mittens—are conveniently grouped in bins and baskets. Bins and baskets are great because they are quicker to build and install than drawers and are usually less expensive than drawer stock. The overall storage concept integrates a balanced mix of doors and open shelving: The former make it convenient to hide clutter, the latter make it easy to find and access stuff quickly on the way out the door.

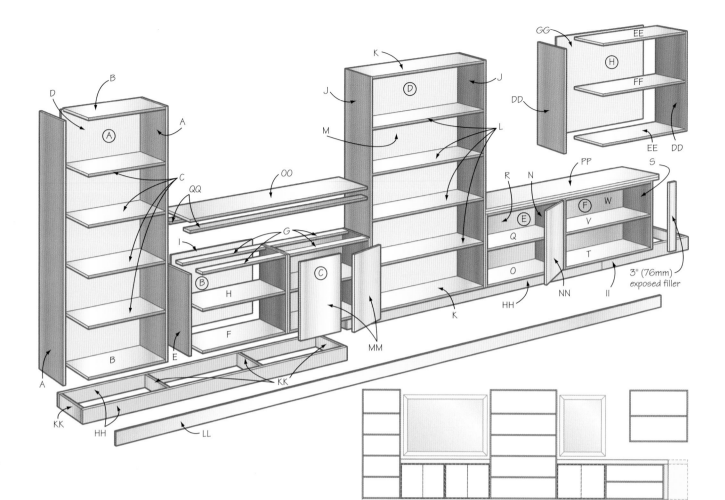

OO

QQ

B
D
A
Ⓐ
C
QQ

A

I
Ⓑ B
H
F
E
B
A

G
G
Ⓒ C
MM
KK
KK
HH
LL

K
J D Ⓓ J
M
L

R N PP S
DD
GG EE
Ⓗ H
FF
EE DD

PP
Ⓔ E W
Q Ⓕ F V
O T
HH NN II
K

3" (76mm)
exposed filler

TT
UU
SKI RACK

PP
RR
Z CC
X
Ⓖ G
AA
Y
BB AA
KK
SS
X
LL
JJ
KK

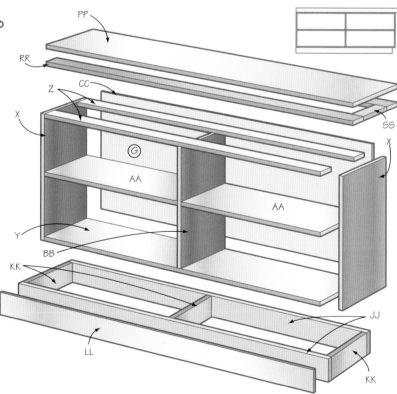

66

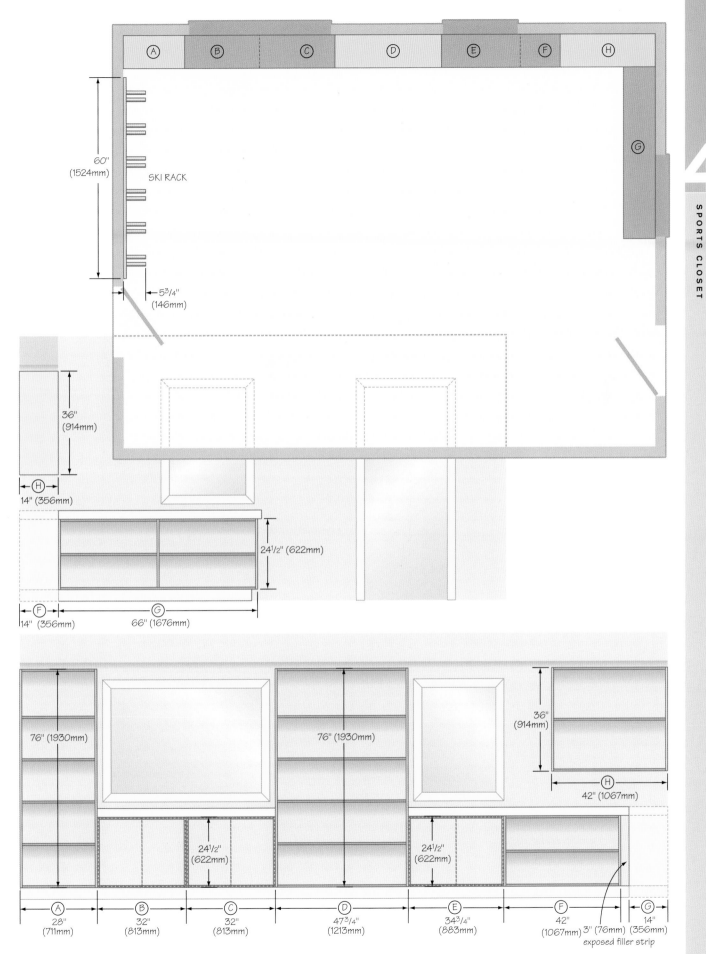

60"
(1524mm)

SKI RACK

5³/₄"
(146mm)

36"
(914mm)

H
14" (356mm)

24¹/₂" (622mm)

F
14" (356mm)

G
66" (1676mm)

36"
(914mm)

76" (1930mm)

76" (1930mm)

H
42" (1067mm)

24¹/₂"
(622mm)

24¹/₂"
(622mm)

A
28"
(711mm)

B
32"
(813mm)

C
32"
(813mm)

D
47³/₄"
(1213mm)

E
34³/₄"
(883mm)

F
42"
(1067mm)

3" (76mm)
exposed filler strip

G
14"
(356mm)

inches (millimeters)

REFERENCE	QUANTITY	PART	STOCK	THICKNESS	(mm)	WIDTH	(mm)	LENGTH	(mm)	COMMENTS
CABINET A										
A	2	sides	plywood	3/4	(19)	14	(356)	76	(1930)	
B	2	top & bottom	plywood	3/4	(19)	14	(356)	26 1/2	(673)	
C	4	shelves	plywood	3/4	(19)	13 1/4	(337)	26 1/4	(667)	
D	1	back	plywood	1/4	(6)	27 1/4	(692)	75 1/4	(1911)	
CABINET B & C										
E	4	sides	plywood	3/4	(19)	13 3/4	(349)	24 1/2	(622)	
F	2	bottoms	plywood	3/4	(19)	13 3/4	(349)	30 1/2	(775)	
G	4	upper stretchers	plywood	3/4	(19)	4	(102)	30 1/2	(775)	
H	2	shelves	plywood	3/4	(19)	13 1/2	(343)	30 1/4	(768)	
I	2	backs	plywood	1/4	(6)	32	(813)	24 1/2	(622)	
CABINET D										
J	2	sides	plywood	3/4	(19)	14	(356)	76	(1930)	
K	2	top & bottom	plywood	3/4	(19)	14	(356)	46 1/4	(1175)	
L	4	shelves	plywood	3/4	(19)	14	(356)	46	(1168)	
M	1	back	plywood	1/4	(6)	47	(1194)	75 1/4	(1911)	
CABINET E										
N	2	sides	plywood	3/4	(19)	13 3/4	(349)	24 1/2	(622)	
O	1	bottom	plywood	3/4	(19)	13 3/4	(349)	33 1/4	(845)	
P	2	upper stretchers	plywood	3/4	(19)	4	(102)	33 1/4	(845)	
Q	1	shelf	plywood	3/4	(19)	13 1/2	(343)	33	(838)	
R	1	back	plywood	1/4	(6)	34 3/4	(883)	24 1/2	(622)	
CABINET F										
S	2	sides	plywood	3/4	(19)	13 3/4	(349)	24 1/2	(622)	
T	1	bottom	plywood	3/4	(19)	13 3/4	(349)	40 1/2	(1029)	
U	2	upper stretchers	plywood	3/4	(19)	4	(102)	40 1/2	(1029)	
V	1	shelf	plywood	3/4	(19)	13 1/2	(343)	40 1/4	(1022)	
W	1	back	plywood	3/4	(19)	42	(1067)	24 1/2	(622)	
CABINET G										
X	2	sides	plywood	3/4	(19)	14	(356)	24 1/2	(622)	
Y	1	bottom	plywood	3/4	(19)	14	(356)	64 1/2	(1638)	
Z	2	upper stretchers	plywood	3/4	(19)	4	(102)	64 1/2	(1638)	
AA	2	shelves	plywood	3/4	(19)	13 1/4	(337)	31 5/8	(803)	
BB	1	vertical divider	plywood	3/4	(19)	13 1/2	(343)	23	(584)	
CC	1	back	plywood	1/4	(6)	23 3/4	(603)	65 1/4	(1657)	
CABINET H										
DD	2	sides	plywood	3/4	(19)	14	(356)	36	(914)	
EE	2	top & bottom	plywood	3/4	(19)	14	(356)	40 1/2	(1029)	
FF	1	shelf	plywood	3/4	(19)	13 1/4	(337)	40 1/4	(1022)	
GG	1	back	plywood	1/4	(6)	41 1/4	(1048)	35 1/4	(895)	
BASES (The lengths for these parts aren't critical, as long as they add up to the required lengths. This is a good chance to use long, narrow scraps.										
HH	4	base fronts & backs	plywood	3/4	(19)	4	(102)	96	(2438)	
II	2	base front & back	plywood	3/4	(19)	4	(102)	30	(762)	
JJ	2	base front & back	plywood	3/4	(19)	4	(102)	66	(1276)	
KK	13	base interior stretchers & sides	plywood	3/4	(19)	4	(102)	9 1/2	(241)	
LL		toe kick trim	plywood	1/4	(6)	16	(406)	25'	(7.6m)	random lenths are OK

inches (millimeters)

REFERENCE	QUANTITY	PART	STOCK	THICKNESS	(mm)	WIDTH	(mm)	LENGTH	(mm)	COMMENTS
DOORS										
MM	4	doors	plywood	$3/4$	(19)	$15^5/8$	(397)	$23^3/4$	(603)	
NN	2	doors	plywood	$3/4$	(19)	17	(432)	$23^3/4$	(603)	
COUNTERTOPS										
OO	1	countertop blank	plywood	$3/4$	(19)	14	(356)	64	(1626)	
PP	2	countertop blanks	plywood	$3/4$	(19)	14	(356)	84	(2134)	
QQ	2	reinforcing strips	plywood	$3/4$	(19)	3	(76)	64	(1626)	
RR	4	reinforcing strips	plywood	$3/4$	(19)	3	(76)	84	(2134)	
SS	1	reinforcing strips	plywood	$3/4$	(19)	3	(76)	8	(203)	for the exposed end
SKI RACK										
TT	1	back plate	plywood	$3/4$	(19)	6	(152)	50	(1270)	
UU	12	dowels	maple	$15/16$	(24)			$5^3/4$	(146)	

component listing

Cabinet A	76" high × 28" wide × 14" × deep (193 × 71 × 36cm)
Cabinet B	$24^1/2$" high × 32" wide × 14" × deep (62 × 81 × 36cm)
Cabinet C	$24^1/2$" high × 32" wide × 14" × deep (62 × 81 × 36cm)
Cabinet D	76" high × $47^3/4$" wide × 14" × deep (193 × 121 × 36cm)
Cabinet E	$24^1/2$" high × $34^3/4$" wide × 14" × deep (62 × 88 × 36cm)
Cabinet F	$24^1/2$" high × 42" wide × 14" × deep (62 × 107 × 36cm)
Cabinet G	$24^1/2$" high × 66" wide × 14" × deep (62 × 168 × 36cm)
Cabinet H	36" high × 42" wide × 14" × deep (91 × 107 × 36cm)
Countertop A:	64" long × 14" deep × $1^1/2$" thick (163 × 36 × 4cm)
Coutnertop B:	84" long × 14" deep × $1^1/2$" thick (213 × 36 × 4cm)
Countertop C:	84" long × 14" deep × $1^1/2$" thick (213 × 36 × 4cm)
Cabinet bases:	2 @ 96" × 11" × 4" (244 × 28 × 10cm)
	1 @ 30" × 11" × 4" (76 × 28 × 10cm)
	1 @ 66" × 11" × 4" (168 × 28 × 10cm)

1 Begin by assembling the cabinet bases with glue and nails. Don't worry about the nail heads being exposed because a piece of trim will cover it later on. You'll also notice that the stretchers are inset to the fronts and backs, which is important because it allows you to use stretchers of the same length for both the sides and the interiors of the bases.

2 This project requires a lot of parts, but most of them are the same width, so it is pretty efficient to cut them all at once. I perform most of my crosscuts with a table-saw sled.

3 The cabinet parts require some work prior to assembly. You can do the edge-banding now or later, but I find it easier to drill the shelf-peg holes early on in the process.

4 The layout of some of these cabinets allows a few shortcuts in their construction. You'll notice that the sides of cabinets B,C,E and F are not exposed. This means you can save some time by just nailing or screwing the cases together.

5 These cabinets can have the backs screwed directly on to the cabinet cases.

6 Cabinets A, D, G and H all have at least one side exposed, so I chose a more refined method of construction for them. On the exposed areas, I used pocket screws instead of through screws. I suggest immediately wiping away glue squeeze-out with a damp paper towel.

7 Instead of nailing or screwing on the back, you can cut a dado into the cabinet parts for the back to nestle into. This takes a little more time but creates a very professional look. Note that the bottom edges of the side panels are visible on cabinet H, so be sure to edge-band them as well.

8 Nail the partition in cabinet G through the top, bottom and back. If it is too snug, use a rubber mallet to ease it into place.

9 The countertops consist of ³/₄" (19mm) plywood that is doubled-up at its edges. Glue and screw down the 4"-wide (102mm) strips for maximum stiffness and durability. The exposed edges can be edge-banded with 2"-wide (51mm) banding when the glue has dried.

10 The doors are made from ³/₄" (19mm) plywood that has been edge-banded on all four sides. The holes for the European-style hinges are located 4" (102mm) from the top/bottom edge of the doors, and ¹⁵/₁₆" (24mm) from the side.

11 If your workshop has enough space, I recommend setting up the components as you will for final assembly. Doing so allows you to see any problems that may have slipped in. And it's generally easier to fix problems while you're still in the shop and have all of your tools at hand. In addition, the final installation will go more smoothly because you have already mocked it up once and you'll know exactly what you're doing. While this may seem like extra work, I cannot stress enough how helpful it can be.

12 The wall-mounted ski rack starts with a back plate. If you're using plywood, you'll want to edge-band all four sides.

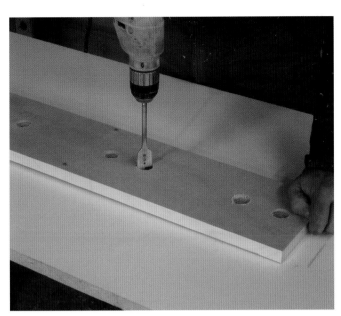

13 This rack will hold six pairs of skis, which means that you'll need to drill six pairs of $^{15}/_{16}$"-diameter (24mm) holes at regular intervals. In this case, I spaced the first hole $1^{1}/_{2}$" (38mm) from the ends, then spaced the pairs 7" (178mm) apart. The centers of the holes are located $2^{1}/_{2}$" (64mm) apart.

14 I recommend sanding the exposed ends of the dowels on a disc sander. This creates a more finished look and also prevents the ends from splintering in the future.

15 The dowels themselves will fit very snugly; tap them in with a few taps from a rubber mallet. Once the glue has set, the rack can be varnished. I recommend a wipe-on urethane because it will provide the easiest way to handle the irregular shapes.

16 I recruited an assistant to help with installation, a good idea for a project of this size. First lay out all the bases and screw them together end to end.

17 I find it easier to level the bases on a long uninterrupted run like this when they are attached. Using a 4' (1219mm) level (or a laser level, if you are so equipped), locate any spots that are out of level and shim accordingly so the entire assembly of bases reads level along its entire length.

18 Level the bases from front to back as well. Doing so makes a huge difference in how the cabinets sit against the wall.

19 Screw the bases into studs in the back wall so they won't move around when you set the cabinets.

20 To install the cabinets, start on the left-hand side of the assembly because there's a more complicated L-shape grouping on the right-hand side which, will require the use of a filler. The cabinets at the left are positioned flush against the wall.

21 Cut holes into the cabinet backs where needed for electrical outlets. A jigsaw does the job quickly and neatly.

22 Screw the cabinets together through their sides, using clamps to line up the front edges. Then screw the cabinets to studs in the wall. A stud finder will help you locate the studs behind the cabinet backs.

23 Taking accurate measurements means everything will fit into place the first time.

24 Screw the wall cabinet to the wall in six places. If you're working alone, you can prop up the cabinet on a milk crate and use some scrap wood to lift it to the right height.

25 Attached the narrow filler to cabinet G, which is also screwed through the back side of the filler that is attached to cabinet F.

26 The countertops are attached to the cabinets with screws from below.

27 Time for the finishing touches. Cut the shims flush with the cabinet bases so the toekick trim can cover them up. I used a Dozuki-style handsaw to make quick work of this.

28 Hanging the doors is straightforward. For detailed information on installing and adjusting european-style hinges, see the sidebar in the Closet-Based Home Office.

29 Screw the ski rack into at least two studs.

building a basic crosscut sled

CUTTING LARGE PLYWOOD PANELS DOWN TO SIZE CAN BE A CHORE, SO IF YOU NEED TO DO A LOT OF IT, I RECOMMEND TAKING THE TIME TO BUILD A CROSSCUT SLED. THE SLED IS COMPOSED OF A $^3/_4$"-THICK (19MM) DECK THAT HAS HARDWOOD RUNNERS GLUED AND SCREWED TO ITS BOTTOM SIDE. THE RUNNERS SLIDE BACK AND FORTH IN THE GROOVES THAT ARE SET INTO THE TOP OF YOUR TABLE SAW, AND YOUR WORKPIECE IS HELD SQUARELY IN PLACE BY A STRIP OF WOOD THAT RUNS ACROSS THE BACK EDGE OF THE DECK. THE SIZE OF THE DECK ISN'T CRITICAL, ALTHOUGH A LARGER DECK WILL ALLOW YOU TO CUT DOWN WIDER PANELS. I SUGGEST 30" × 48" (762MM × 1219MM) AS A GOOD STARTING POINT.

You'll want to start by milling two strips of hardwood that fit into the grooves on the table-saw top—they should move easily from front to back, but they should have very little side to side movement. The strips should be about $^1/_{16}$" (2mm) higher than the table-saw top.

My shortcut for aligning the strips to the deck is simple and requires no measurement. With the strips positioned in their grooves, I put some 5-minute epoxy on top of them, then place the deck on top. When the epoxy has cured, the nearly completed sled should move back and forth easily. If it is a tight fit, you can trim the runners with a sharp chisel or rabbeting plane. For durability, I suggest countersinking a few screws through the runners into the bottom of the deck.

I recommend attaching a 2×4 or 2×6 brace to the front edge of the sled for stability. You can glue and screw it without worrying about an exact position. The brace at the back edge of the sled, however, must be placed square to the blade. To determine its placement, retract the blade completely into the saw and raise it slowly to cut a kerf across most of the sled's top. You won't want to cut it completely from front to back, since the sled would just fall apart at this point—if you cut about 18" (457mm) or more, you'll be able to lay a framing square along the kerf and mark a perpendicular edge at the back of the sled. I recommend flipping over the square and marking lines on both the right and left of the kerf. This should provide a straight line along which to align the rear brace. Then glue and screw the brace for stability, and cut all the way through the deck from front to back.

walk-in closet

This is a dream closet for

these homeowners. The long wall provided
an opportunity for a focal point, so we embel-
lished it with framed artwork, fresh flowers
and accent lighting. We also chose to place
the clothes rods on the side walls so the carefully composed look of the focal wall would
be as uncluttered as possible. The doors and
drawer fronts display a shop-made molding
detail, and the drawers, which feature velvet drawer bottoms and hardwood dividers,
are made to contain jewelry. We used fluted
molding and rosettes for some of the trim,
and a medium-toned stain to complement
the neutral wall color. The small countertop
area is tiled in limestone, and crown molding
caps off the top of the organizer.

From a functional point of view, this closet
presents a question that is unique to walk-
in closets: how to best use the space in the
corners of the room. This design incorpo-
rates corner units to take advantage of the
available space and make it as accessible
as possible. Each unit is built as one solid
piece, thereby providing a great deal of stability. This project was built with 3/4" (19mm)
okume plywood, an African mahogany sub-
stitute.

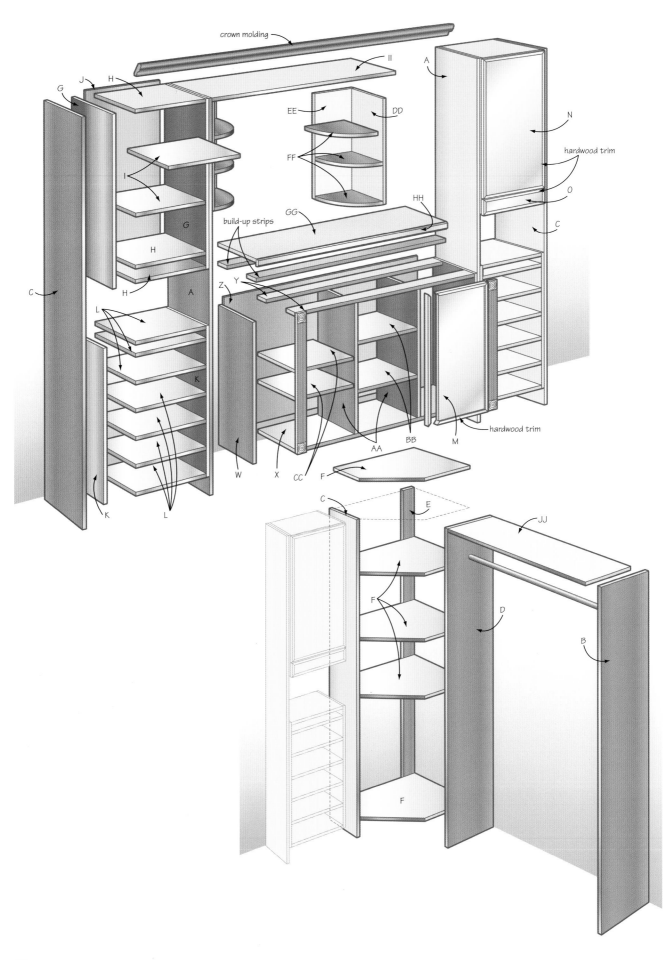

crown molding

II

A

J H

G

EE

DD

N

hardwood trim

FF

O

HH

C

build-up strips

GG

I

G

H

H

A

Z Y

L

A

K

BB

M

hardwood trim

C

W

AA

K

X CC

F

L

C

E

F

JJ

D

B

F

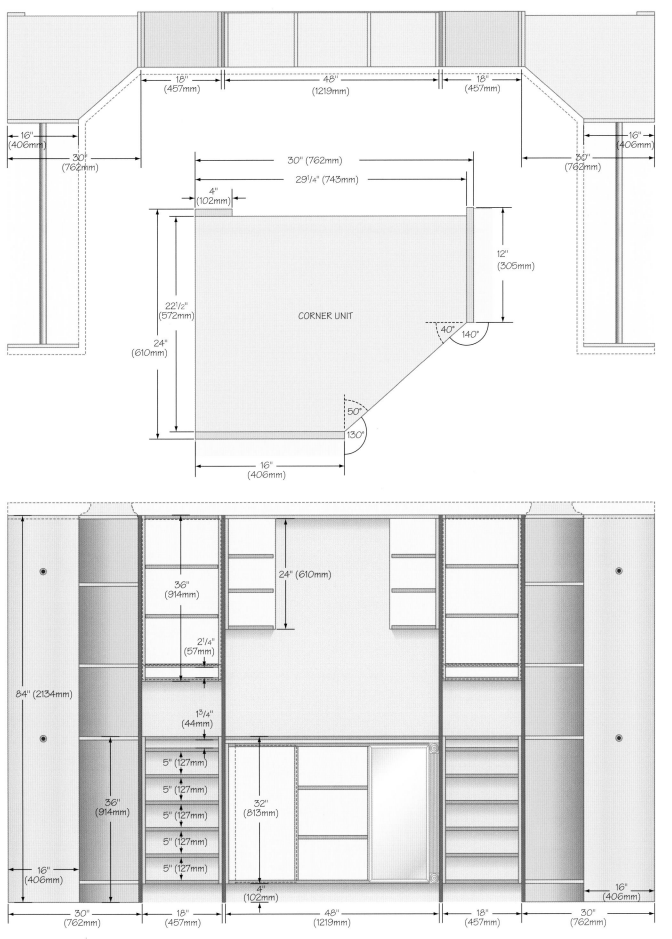

18"
(457mm)

48"
(1219mm)

18"
(457mm)

16"
(406mm)

30"
(762mm)

30"
(762mm)

16"
(406mm)

30" (762mm)

29¹/₄" (743mm)

4"
(102mm)

12"
(305mm)

22¹/₂"
(572mm)

24"
(610mm)

CORNER UNIT

40° 140°

50°

130°

16"
(406mm)

84" (2134mm)

36"
(914mm)

24" (610mm)

2¹/₄"
(57mm)

1³/₄"
(44mm)

5" (127mm)

5" (127mm)

5" (127mm)

5" (127mm)

5" (127mm)

36"
(914mm)

32"
(813mm)

4"
(102mm)

16"
(406mm)

16"
(406mm)

30"
(762mm)

18"
(457mm)

48"
(1219mm)

18"
(457mm)

30"
(762mm)

inches (millimeters)

REFERENCE	QUANTITY	PART	STOCK	THICKNESS	(mm)	WIDTH	(mm)	LENGTH	(mm)
A	2	end panels	plywood	$3/4$	(19)	12	(305)	84	(2134)
B	2	end panels	plywood	$3/4$	(19)	16	(406)	84	(2134)
CORNER UNITS									
C	2	sides	plywood	$3/4$	(19)	12	(305)	84	(2134)
D	2	sides	plywood	$3/4$	(19)	16	(406)	84	(2134)
E	2	vertical support strips	plywood	$3/4$	(19)	4	(102)	70	(1778)
F	10	tops, bottoms, fixed shelves	plywood	$3/4$	(19)	$22^1/2$	(572)	$29^1/4$	(743)
UPPER CABINETS									
G	4	sides	plywood	$3/4$	(19)	$11^3/4$	(298)	36	(914)
H	4	tops & bottoms	plywood	$3/4$	(19)	$11^3/4$	(298)	$16^1/2$	(419)
I	4	floating shelves	plywood	$3/4$	(19)	$11^1/2$	(292)	$16^1/4$	(413)
J	2	backs	plywood	$1/4$	(6)	18	(457)	36	(914)
SHOE CUBBIES									
K	4	sides	plywood	$3/4$	(19)	12	(305)	32	(813)
L	14	tops, bottoms, fixed shelves	plywood	$3/4$	(19)	12	(305)	$16^1/2$	(419)
CABINET DOORS & DRAWER FRONTS									
M	2	door panels	plywood	$3/4$	(19)	$16^1/4$	(413)	30	(762)
N	2	door panels	plywood	$3/4$	(19)	$12^1/4$	(311)	$28^1/4$	(718)
O	2	drawer front panels	plywood	$3/4$	(19)	3	(76)	$16^1/4$	(413)
P	8	trim for panels	hardwood	$3/4$	(19)	$1^1/2$	(38)	32	(813)
Q	8	trim for panels	hardwood	$3/4$	(19)	$1^1/2$	(38)	18	(457)
R	4	trim for panels	hardwood	$3/4$	(19)	$1^1/2$	(38)	15	(381)
S	4	trim for panels	hardwood	$3/4$	(19)	$1^1/2$	(38)	5	(127)
T	4	drawer sides	plywood	$1/2$	(13)	3	(76)	11	(279)
U	4	drawer fronts & backs	plywood	$1/2$	(13)	3	(76)	$14^1/2$	(368)
V	2	drawer bottoms	plywood	$1/4$	(6)	$10^1/2$	(267)	14	(356)
BASE CABINET									
W	2	sides	plywood	$3/4$	(19)	$11^3/4$	(298)	31	(787)
X	1	bottom	plywood	$3/4$	(19)	$11^3/4$	(298)	$46^1/2$	(1181)
Y	2	top stretchers	plywood	$3/4$	(19)	4	(102)	$46^1/2$	(1181)
Z	1	back	plywood	$1/4$	(6)	31	(787)	48	(1219)
AA	2	vertical partitions	plywood	$3/4$	(19)	$11^3/4$	(298)	$29^1/2$	(750)
BB	3	fixed shelves	plywood	$3/4$	(19)	$11^3/4$	(298)	$15^1/2$	(394)
CC	4	floating shelves	plywood	$3/4$	(19)	$11^3/4$	(298)	$12^1/4$	(311)
CURVED SHELF UNITS									
DD	2	sides & backs	plywood	$3/4$	(19)	$10^1/2$	(267)	30	(762)
EE	2	sides & backs	plywood	$3/4$	(19)	$11^1/4$	(286)	30	(762)
FF	8	curved shelves	plywood	$3/4$	(19)	10	(254)	10	(254)
MISCELLANEOUS PARTS									
GG	1	countertop	plywood	$3/4$	(19)	12	(305)	48	(1219)
HH	1	countertop trim	hardwood	$3/4$	(19)	$1^3/4$	(44)	48	(1219)
II	1	header	plywood	$3/4$	(19)	12	(305)	48	(1219)
JJ	2	upper shelves above rods	plywood	$3/4$	(19)	16	(406)	48	(1219)

hardware & supplies

1	96" (2438mm) crown molding
2	27" (686mm) crown molding
2	54" (1372mm) crown molding
1	accent light
2 sets	undermount drawer slides (10" long (250mm), full extension)
6	drawer pulls
3	48" (1219mm) hanging rods
3 sets	hanging rod support hardware
2	24"×16" (610 × 406mm) pieces of velvet for jewelry drawer bottoms
	5mm shelf pegs
	$7/8$" (22mm) edge-banding
4	limestone tiles @ 12"×12"× $1/4$" thick (305 × 305 × 6mm) (optional)
	60" (1524mm) fluted molding
2	decorative rosettes
2	decorative corner blocks

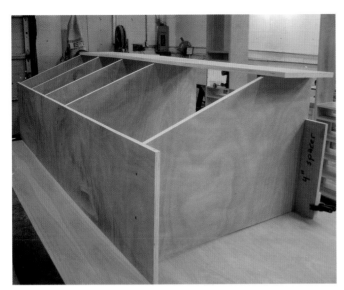

1 Begin with the corner units. You'll notice that they are not symmetrical. This is because the units on the long wall are 12" (305mm) deep, but the units on the short walls where the clothes rods go are 16" (406mm) deep to accommodate hanging garments. This doesn't pose any problems in construction but it is an important aspect of the design. The shelves are fixed into place with screws. Note: It is a lot easier to edge-band the shelves before assembling the corner units.

2 Rip and crosscut the parts for the base cabinet, then assemble it with screws. The screw heads won't show, since end panels will cover the sides of the cabinet. We dressed up the cabinets with some trim from a local home center. The trim consists of a length of fluted molding, a rosette and a plinth. The parts are glued and nailed to the cabinet, and the nail holes are later filled with a stainable putty. Screw the two vertical partitions from the top, bottom and back.

3 You'll notice that because the trim pieces overhang in the body of the cabinet they could be easily damaged if they're not reinforced. I put in two bracing strips.

4 We fixed the shelves in the middle bay to accommodate a set of baskets we planned to use.

5 The end panels are screwed directly to the cabinet. The screw heads won't show if you screw from the outside because other cabinets will cover them later. Use a 4" (102mm) spacer to postion the end panels accurately.

6 The header has several functions: it serves as a place to mount the overhead lights, it provides a place to securely fasten the crown molding and it helps to create a more built-in look.

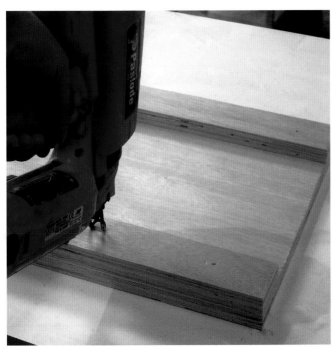

7 This countertop begins with a 48" × 12" (1219mm × 305mm) blank. I built up the edges with $^3/_4$"-thick (19mm) strips of plywood to give it a more substantial look.

8 Since this was a pretty elegant project, I decided to tile the top with 12" × 12" (305mm × 305mm) limestone. That meant installing a $1^3/_4$"-wide (44mm) trim strip for the front edge, because the tiles are $^1/_4$" (6mm) thick. If you're doing a standard wooden top, make the trim strip $1^1/_2$" (44mm) wide. I routed the top and bottom edges of the strip on the router table.

9 Attach the strip with glue and nails. For a tile top, you must raise the strip $^1/_4$" (6mm) to conceal the front edge of the tiles.

16 Install the corner units first.

17 The shoe cubby and the upper cabinet are screwed to the side of the corner unit. Since I took the time to mock up the installation in the shop, they are easy to align—use the screw holes to set the components exactly into place.

18 I had an assistant for this installation, so I was able to assemble the center unit in my shop, then transfer it to the closet, which saved some time.

19 The shoe cubby and the upper cabinet to the right of the base cabinet can be reattached now. I used a 4" (102mm) spacer to establish the height of the shoe cubby.

20 Screw the clothes rods directly onto the side panel of the corner unit. Notice that I attached a cleat above the clothes rod so the upper shelf has a place to land. The upper shelf isn't designed to support heavy objects, although you could easily reinforce it, if desired. Its main function is to provide a place to attach the crown molding.

21 Cutting and installing crown molding is too big a topic to fully get into here, but I can at least point you to a great book on the subject: *Crown Molding and Trim, Install It Like a Pro* (Universal Publishers). I used an angle gauge to determine the angles where the components come together, then consulted the book to find the settings for my compound miter saw.

22 Accent lighting is a nice touch. This unit didn't require an electrician: It plugs into an existing outlet.

laundry room closet

This laundry center provides some neat ways to get

a lot done in a small space. It is a great example of how you can design an area
to be both highly functional and aesthetically pleasing. The original configuration had sliding doors, which were cumbersome and only allowed access to one
half of the closet at a time. By replacing them with conventional hinged doors,
we opened up the space and made it more practical and inviting.

The flip-down ironing board is a great space and timer saver: No more dragging
out the old clunker and setting it up in the middle of the room (where it would
invariably be in someone's way!) We had initially considered integrating an
ironing board in one of the cabinets inside the closet, but we realized that this
would mean taking up space that could be better used for storing sheets and
towels. We achieved the best of all worlds by installing the ironing board on the
back of one of the closet doors. You'll also notice that the cabinet to the left of
the washer/dryer is raised 20" (508mm) from the floor to allow a laundry basket
to nest beneath it. This frees up precious floor space while the laundry center is
being used.

We used ¾" (19mm) melamine-covered particleboard for this project. Melamine
is a water-resistant, easy-to-care for material, and because it is white, it reflects
light, keeping the closet interior bright with a roomy feel.

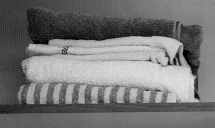
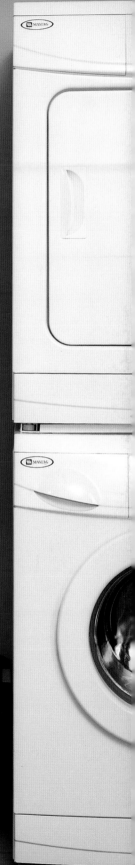

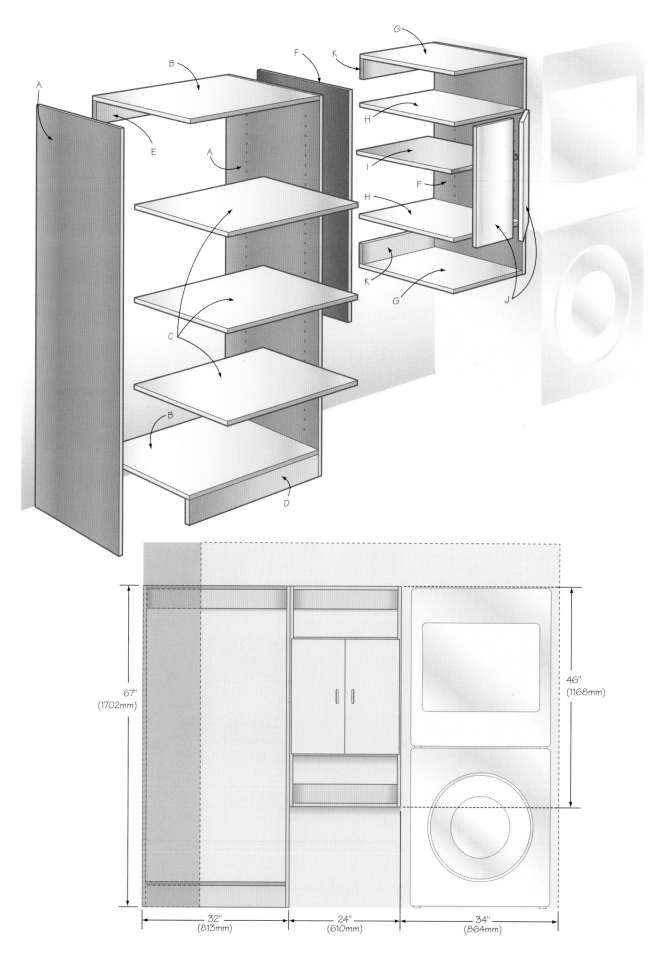

A

B

F

K

G

E

A

H

H

I

F

C

B

J

G

K

D

67"
(1702mm)

46"
(1168mm)

32"
(813mm)

24"
(610mm)

34"
(864mm)

inches (millimeters)

REFERENCE	QUANTITY	PART	STOCK	THICKNESS	(mm)	WIDTH	(mm)	LENGTH	(mm)
LARGE CABINET									
A	2	sides	melamine	3/4	(19)	16	(406)	67	(1702)
B	2	top & bottom	melamine	3/4	(19)	16	(406)	30 1/2	(775)
C	3	floating shelves	melamine	3/4	(19)	16	(406)	30 1/4	(768)
D	1	toe kick	melamine	3/4	(19)	4 1/2	(114)	30 1/2	(775)
E	1	back wall stretcher	melamine	3/4	(19)	4	(102)	30 1/2	(775)
SMALL CABINET									
F	2	sides	melamine	3/4	(19)	16	(406)	36	(914)
G	2	top and bottom	melamine	3/4	(19)	16	(406)	22 1/2	(572)
H	2	fixed shelves	melamine	3/4	(19)	16	(406)	22 1/2	(572)
I	1	floating shelf	melamine	3/4	(19)	15 3/4	(400)	22 1/4	(565)
J	2	cabinet doors	cherry ply	3/4	(19)	11 3/8	(289)	24	(610)
K	2	back wall stretchers	melamine	3/4	(19)	4	(102)	22 1/2	(572)

hardware & supplies

4	hinges and mounting plates (35mm), full overlay, with 3mm plates
2	door pulls
1	over-the-door ironing door (see supplier's list page 12)
20	5mm shelf pegs
	7/8"-wide (22mm) cherry edge-banding

1 Build the smaller, wall-hung cabinet first. I cut the parts to size using my table saw and a blade specifically meant for cutting melamine. While most any combination blade will provide acceptable results, melamine-specific blades tend to produce the smallest amount of tear-out.

2 Using a template, drill holes on the side panels for the 5mm shelf pegs.

3 I decided to use cherry edge-banding on this project because it coordinated nicely with the cherry doors and because it functioned as a common element which helped to unify the different components in the design. I used a razor blade to remove the excess. You'll get a fast, clean cut if you hold the back edge of the blade at a slight angle and pull it firmly towards you.

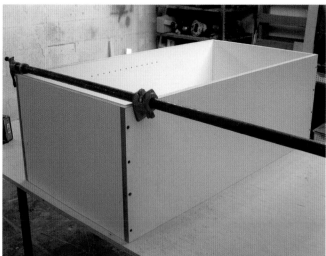

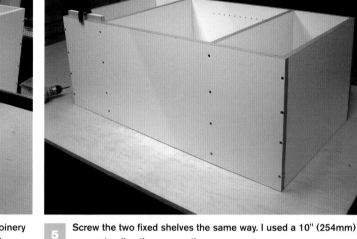

4 Your tools and your personal preference will determine the joinery methods you use here. I went with countersunk screws, as they hold very well in particleboard when pilot holes are predrilled and an appropriate adhesive is used. I have recently become a fan of Roo Glue's adhesive for melamine. I wouldn't consider building with melamine without it (see Suppliers at the back of the book). The assembly is straightforward. Work on one corner at a time and use clamps to hold the panels in place. The screw heads won't be visible on this cabinet, so don't worry about filling or covering them.

5 Screw the two fixed shelves the same way. I used a 10" (254mm) spacer to align them correctly.

6 The back wall stretchers provide a place to screw the cabinet into the studs in the wall. I placed them inside the portion of cabinet that will be hidden by the doors. Doing so makes for a less cluttered look when the cabinet is installed.

7 I made the doors from some scrap cherry plywood. (You can use the species of wood you desire.) Use a $1^{3}/_{8}$" (35mm) Forstner bit to drill the hinge holes 4" (102mm) from the top and bottom edges of the doors, and $^{13}/_{16}$" (21mm) in from the edges.

8 Screw the hinge cups into the doors themselves, and screw the hinge plates, with the doors attached, onto the cabinet sides. With only two doors, this is an easy task.

10 The larger cabinet is essentially an open-backed bookcase. I left the back off as a way to save money. In general, moving cabinets puts a lot of stress on their joints, and a back would provide considerable strength. Because this cabinet will be transported only once, and because it will be screwed into place and never moved again, this is a perfectly reasonable option. I cut the parts to size on my table-saw sled, then edge-banded them and drilled the shelf peg holes just as I did for the small cabinet.

9 An inexpensive template (available at most home centers) makes for quick and consistent layout of the door pulls. You can see that the grain of the doors matches nicely—this is because they came from the same piece of plywood.

11 I used pocket screws to hold the bottom in place. I chose pocket screws because I wanted the exposed screw heads on the bottom right side of the piece to be concealed. Fastcap self-stick screw head covers would've helped, but pocket screws are equally quick and look even better.

12 I also attached the toekick with pocket screws where they'll be hidden from view. The toekick is set in $1/2$" (13mm) from the front edge of the cabinet.

13 Once the fixed shelf and the top have been installed, attach the back wall stretcher in place with some countersunk screws.

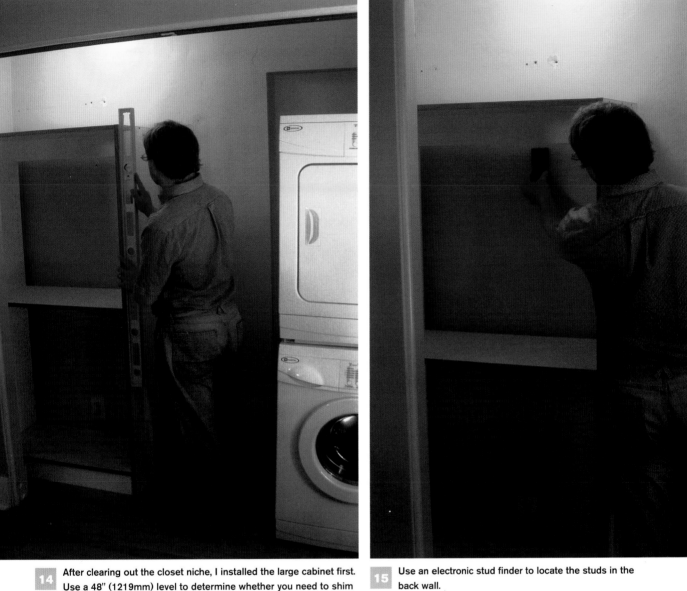

14 After clearing out the closet niche, I installed the large cabinet first. Use a 48" (1219mm) level to determine whether you need to shim the cabinet to make it plumb and level.

15 Use an electronic stud finder to locate the studs in the back wall.

16
I recommend using two 3" (76mm) cabinet screws per stud.

17 Since I performed the installation by myself, I built a temporary stand for the wall-hung cabinet. It consists of two plywood scraps that I nailed together in the shape of a T, and it provided all the support necessary to keep the cabinet in place while I fastened it to the wall.

18 For some wiggle room, build the temporary support ¹/₄" (6mm) shorter than the finished height. I used shims to align the top edges of the cabinets.

19 Once the front edges of the cabinets are screwed together with 1¹/₄" (32mm) self-tapping screws, the separate units will start to read as one unit. If you took the time to mock up the installation in the shop, as I did, the screw holes will already be in the right places and this step will be a snap. Either way, I suggest using a quick-clamp to hold the edges flush while you're putting in the screws.

20 Screw the smaller cabinet to the back wall, and remove the shims and temporary support.

21 The 35mm hinges make it easy to reattach the doors on site. I generally remove them while cabinets are in transit to avoid damaging them. You may need to make a couple of minor on-site adjustments to make the doors hang evenly, but it should only take a couple of minutes.

kids closet

Zack and Max, age 7 and 4, share a large bedroom which is equipped with two large closets. The overall plan dedicates one closet to the storage of toys and games and the other to clothing. This project tackles the clothing storage closet. The homeowners desired a symmetrical arrangement, so that each boy would have an identical space, and neither would be favored or slighted by a better or worse allocation of space. You'll notice the design centers on a vertical axis that divides the space into two mirror images.

This reach-in closet has a 60"-wide (1524mm) entry and about 18" (457mm) of space on either side of the doorway. Hence, most of the contents of the closet are readily visible, which makes the whole system easier to use. The less visible areas to the sides of the closet can be reserved for seasonal storage or less frequently used items. We decided to use the areas in the bottom corners for shoe caddies, so that shoes don't end up all over the floor, and we raised the drawer unit 18" (457mm) to accommodate a shared laundry basket. Each boy has the same amount of drawer, shelf and hanging rod space, and the bottom couple of drawers are at a very accessible height to boys of their young age. As they get older, the higher reaches of the closet will become more accessible and useful. We used adjustable shelves to allow for changing storage needs in the future.

The unit is a neutral color—since the boys have plenty of colorful clothing as it is, we wanted to avoid the visual chaos that could easily result from bright, childish colors. The neutral color will still be appropriate when the boys are older.

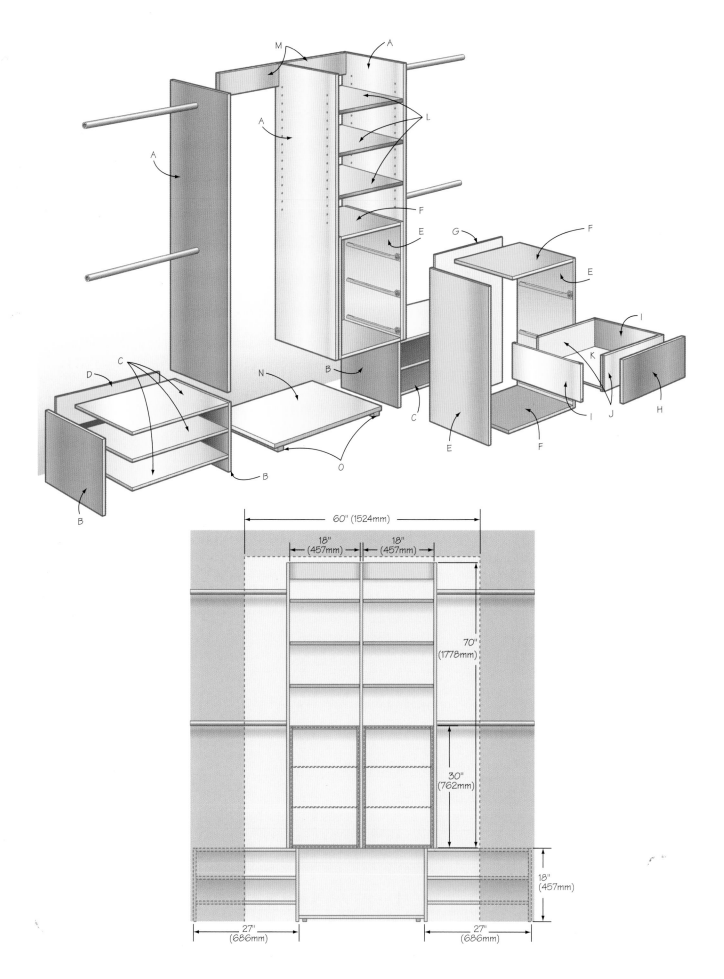

inches (millimeters)

REFERENCE	QUANTITY	PART	STOCK	THICKNESS	(mm)	WIDTH	(mm)	LENGTH	(mm)
A	3	end panels	MDF	¾	(19)	16	(406)	70	(1778)
SHOE CUBBIES (2)									
B	4	sides	MDF	¾	(19)	15¾	(400)	18	(457)
C	6	tops and shelves	MDF	¾	(19)	15¾	(400)	25½	(648)
D	2	backs	MDF	¼	(6)	18	(457)	27	(686)
DRAWER UNITS (2)									
E	4	sides	MDF	¾	(19)	15¾	(400)	30	(762)
F	4	tops/bottoms	MDF	¾	(19)	15¾	(400)	16½	(419)
G	2	backs	MDF	¼	(6)	18	(457)	30	(762)
H	6	drawer fronts	MDF	¾	(19)	9⅝	(244)	17¼	(438)
I	12	drawer sides	MDF	½	(13)	8½	(216)	15½	(394)
J	12	drawer fronts and backs	MDF	½	(13)	8½	(216)	15½	(394)
K	6	drawer bottoms	MDF	¼	(6)	16	(406)	16	(406)
DRAWER UNITS (2)									
L	6	floating shelves	MDF	¾	(19)	16	(406)	17¾	(451)
M	2	back wall stretchers	MDF	¾	(19)	4	(102)	18	(457)
N	1	low shelf	MDF	¾	(19)	16	(406)	32	(813)
O	2	strut supports	MDF	¾	(19)	1	(25)	32	(813)

hardware & supplies

6 sets	undermount drawer slides (14" (355mm) long, three-quarter extension)
6	drawer pulls
4	30" (762mm) hanging rods
4 sets	hanging rod support hardware
24	5mm shelf pegs

1 Begin by cutting out the parts for the dresser units. I used MDF because it takes paint well and requires no edge-banding, a detail which saves a considerable amount of time. You'll notice that some of the material I used is veneered with alder. I used it only because I got a good deal on it and was able to position those components in such a way that they wouldn't be visible after installation. It's also a good idea to cut out the three end panels at this time, since you're set up for it.

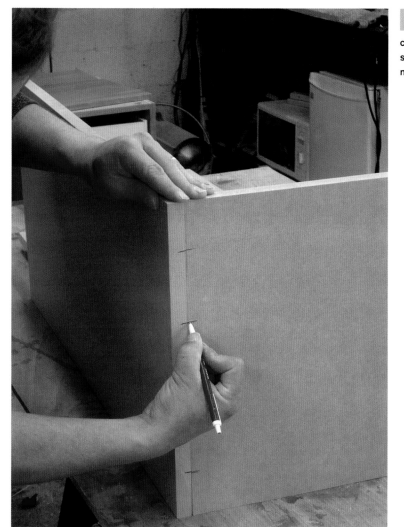

2 The dresser units are constructed with biscuits. I clamped up the units without glue so that I could lay out a series of marks for the biscuits at each joint.

3 The slots in the top and bottom panels are cut with the biscuit joiner held parallel to the workpieces.

4 Cutting the biscuit slots into the side panels is a bit trickier, as the biscuit joiner is positioned perpendicular to the workpiece. I was able to keep the panels steady by placing them on the floor.

5 After a test-fit to make sure the slots are properly aligned, I glued up the assemblies and applied even clamping pressure. The test-fit may seem like a waste of time, but it's not. If you discover a discrepancy in the fit, you'll save a lot of time, stress and mess if you catch it before there's glue all over the place.

6 I attached the ¼''-thick (6mm) back to the dresser unit with glue and screws. You may opt to use brads.

7 When the glue has cured, remove the clamps and sand the joints flush on the top. This will be visible in the finished closet, so a smooth, uniform surface is ideal here. Any gaps can be filled with putty and resanded. I used 60- and 80-grit paper to sand down large discrepancies.

8 Paint the dresser units before installing the drawers to avoid getting paint on the drawers and sliders. The only parts that need paint are the tops and the front edges, as the drawers will hide the insides and the end panels will conceal the outsides.

9 Painting the parts of the shoe cubbies prior to assembly is a must—the tight corners and small spaces are really tough to finish otherwise. When the paint was dry, I used a $5^{1}/_{4}$" (133mm) spacer to align the shelves consistenly. After the assembly is complete, sand the joints and touch them up as needed.

10 Fill all visible screw holes with a non-shrinking putty, then paint.

12 These fairly simple drawers are built with $1/2"$ (13mm) material that's glued and nailed at the corners. The bottoms fit into a groove I ripped near the bottom edge of the drawer stock.

11 This step is optional, but I highly recommend it. Like most of the projects in this book, this closet consists of several components, and I like to put them together in the shop before installation so I can troubleshoot any unforeseen problems. In the event of an installation glitch, I'd much rather be in a well-equipped shop than on a job site where I might not have the resources I need to make corrections. This step also has the beneficial effect of making the installations go much more smoothly. In this case, screw the center end panel to the dresser units, then add the two end panels on the left and right sides. With the help of an assistant, lift the whole assembly onto the shoe cubbies. Be sure to overlap only about 1" (25mm) onto the cubbies so the weight transfers down directly to the floor. Once you screw the unit to the wall during the final installation, the entire thing will be perfectly stable.

13 I used three-quarter extension drawer slides for this project. Install the cabinet-side slides in the cabinets first.

14 With the drawers placed upside down on a workbench, it's easy to install the drawer-side runners with self-tapping $^1/_2$" (13mm) screws. Then you can set the drawers into the cabinet whenever you're ready.

15 I detailed the front edges of the MDF drawer fronts using a $^3/_8$" (10mm) roundover bit. This detail looks nice and eliminates the chipping that often occurs on edges left at 90°. Drawer fronts can be a high-wear area.

17 Because the holes for the chosen drawer pulls required unique spacing, I made my own alignment guide and I used it for all six drawers.

16 The roundover also makes it easier to align the drawer fronts because it conceals slight unevenness between adjacent drawers.

18 You can cut and paint the MDF shelves at any time. I like to mount them on L brackets because you can run a screw through the brackets to lock the shelves in position.

tip Hopefully everything will go smoothly for you during installation, but if it doesn't you might need to practice some creative problem solving, as I did for this particular project. Before I put in the new organizer, I had to remove the old one, which revealed an unforeseen snag. The photo shows a pair of tracks on the floor where carpeting had been installed around the old vertical supports. We realized that the carpet would be impossible to repair, so I decided to cover up the area entirely with a low shelf. The laundry basket still slides in and out, as we originally planned. The finished effect is really nice, and it looks as though it was planned this way all along. So don't panic when a job site hands you a surprise. Sometimes it turns out for the best.

The struts are glued and nailed to the bottom of the shelf. Their role is primarily aesthetic—the shelf looks better when it is elevated slightly above the floor.

19 The shoe cubbies are placed 32" (813mm) apart on the floor. They should be centered on the door opening, since this is a symmetrical organizer.

20 Set the left-hand drawer unit in place. I kept the end panel screwed to its side to save a step, and if I had had an assistant to help me lift it, I would've kept the entire upper assembly (both drawer units and all three end panels) screwed together. That would've saved even more time.

21 The right-hand drawer unit, with end panels attached to both sides, goes in next. Align the front edges, then clamp them together with a quick-clamp. The clamp stabilizes the assembly so you can screw it together.

22 Screw the drawer units into studs in the back wall. I used 12 screws, which may be more than necessary, but better safe than sorry.

23 Prior to loading the parts in the van, I removed the drawers from the preassembled installation. As I removed them, I labeled them according to their position in the finished unit—it would be easy to get them mixed up otherwise. The clothes rods were easy to install. For the drywall anchors, I used 3" (76mm) toggle bolts because there weren't any studs where I needed them.

hall closet

8

I'm using the term hall closet to refer to any closet
located near a home's main entrance—it may or may not actually be in a hall-
way. Not everyone is lucky enough to have one, but for those who do, this
closet can provide a convenient place to store all kinds of stuff. Typical contents
include coats, shoes and umbrellas, and sometimes the vacuum cleaner as well.
There is no one-size-fits-all approach to hall closets: The project here reflects a
custom solution to some unique storage needs.

In this case, closets in other parts of the home handled shoe storage so that
was a nonissue. The amount of coat storage provided in the original configuration was adequate, but the clothes rod was placed at the wrong height for this
family's needs. At eye level, it meant there was only mediocre storage above
and below the coats. We decided to raise the rod to 75" (1905mm) and to create
a large storage area below the coats. This left a 16"-high (406mm) space above,
where we installed a shelf. It's a bit too high to reach on a daily basis but provides extra storage for infrequently used items.

We decided to build a cabinet to fill the area below the coats. It spans most of
the closet's width, with a small space reserved on each side for long coats. The
unit features two pullout drawers for hats and mittens, and an open shelf at the
top for a set of music books the family often uses when they gather around the
piano. They wanted the books to be close at hand without cluttering up the liv-
ing room, and the closet turned out to be an ideal solution.

The unit is freestanding, and it is finished on all sides, which means it can be
removed and used elsewhere, boasting great versatility.

118

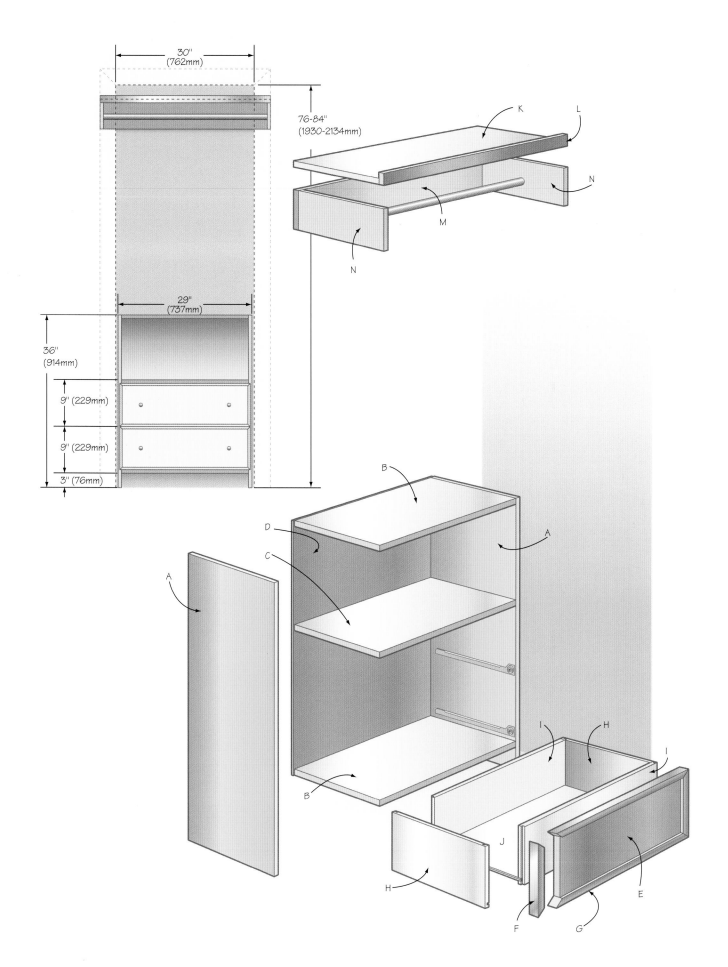

30"
(762mm)

76-84"
(1930-2134mm)

29"
(737mm)

36"
(914mm)

9" (229mm)

9" (229mm)

3" (76mm)

K

L

N

M

N

B

D

A

C

A

I

H

I

B

J

H

F

G

E

inches (millimeters)

REFERENCE	QUANTITY	PART	STOCK	THICKNESS	(mm)	WIDTH	(mm)	LENGTH	(mm)
A	2	sides	oak ply	3/4	(19)	12	(305)	36	(914)
B	2	top/bottom	oak ply	3/4	(19)	12	(305)	27 1/2	(699)
C	1	fixed shelf	oak ply	3/4	(19)	11 1/2	(292)	27 1/2	(699)
D	1	back	oak ply	1/4	(6)	28	(711)	32	(813)
E	2	drawer fronts	oak ply	3/4	(19)	8	(203)	27 1/4	(692)
F	4	drawer front trim	oak	1/2	(13)	7/8	(22)	11	(279)
G	4	drawer front trim	oak	1/2	(13)	7/8	(22)	30	(762)
H	4	drawer sides	birch ply	1/2	(13)	7	(178)	11	(279)
I	4	drawer fronts and backs	birch ply	1/2	(13)	7	(178)	26	(660)
J	2	drawer bottoms	birch ply	1/4	(6)	10 1/2	(267)	26	(660)
K	1	upper shelf	oak ply	3/4	(19)	12	(305)	37	(940)
L	1	front edge shelf edge trim	oak	3/4	(19)	1 1/2	(38)	37	(940)
M	1	back wall cleat	oak ply	3/4	(19)	5 1/2	(140)	37	(940)
N	2	side wall cleats	oak ply	3/4	(19)	5 1/2	(140)	11 1/4	(286)

hardware & supplies

2 sets	10" (255mm) drawer slides (three-quarter extension)
4	drawer pulls
	7/8"-wide (22mm) oak edge-banding
1 set	4 leveling feet
1 set	hanging rod support hardware
1	35 1/4" long steel hanging rod

1 Rip and crosscut the panels to size. If I have a number of pieces that have already been ripped to the same width, I often screw a hold-down style clamp to my table-saw sled to keep the workpieces from moving around. This facilitates safe and accurate crosscutting.

2 The sides, top and bottom are all grooved to hold the 1/4" (6mm) oak plywood back. I used a router table and a straight-cutting bit.

3 Once the groove has been cut, edge-band the parts. This sequence is important because the edge-banding covers up the groove that shows through on the ends of the plywood.

4 I used pocket-hole joinery for this piece.

5 The top gets sandwiched between the sides. Locate the pocket holes on the bottom side where they are out of sight.

6 The back should slide in easily without excess force. Test-fit prior to applying the glue.

7 The bottom is sandwiched between the sides, just like the top. To position it correctly, measure down 3" (76mm) from the bottom edge of the sides and make a couple of small marks in pencil.

8 The center shelf is installed with pocket screws. Measure up 21$\frac{1}{4}$" (540mm) from the bottom edge of the side panels and align the top side of the shelf accordingly.

9 I made a matched pair of edged-panel drawer fronts for this piece. I created the molding profile with a $\frac{1}{4}$" (6mm) roundover bit. The bottom edge of the cutter was raised to $1\frac{1}{16}$" (27mm) below the top of the router table. For more details on this construction method, see Beyond the Basic Box.

10 A cleat along the back of the wall and shorter cleats to either side support the upper shelf and the coat rod. Rip cleats from plywood, then edge-band the edges that will remain visible after the installation.

11 Attach a hardwood strip to the front edge of the upper shelf. It will keep the shelf from sagging over time. I used the same router bit to profile the hardwood strip as I did for the drawer fronts. Doing so provides for nice continuity between components.

12 I used a rich walnut stain for this project. You can use whatever best suits your closet and its surroundings.

13 These aren't deep drawers, so full extension slides were a necessity. For details on drawer slide installation, see the Shared Master Bedroom Closet project. I constructed the drawers using rabbet-and-dado joinery– this is detailed in Beyond the Basic Box.

14 The brushed nickel drawer pulls are great accents to the dark stain.

15 This installation was easy. I removed the old shelf and coat rod first (note the primer on the wall where they used to be). Once the primer dried, I touched up the paint to conceal all traces of the old unit. Then I screwed the back wall cleat to studs.

16 I next screwed the side wall cleats into studs. Once I dropped the shelf into place and screwed in the coat rod, I vacuumed the closet and set the cabinet into place.

suppliers

ADAMS & KENNEDY – THE WOOD SOURCE
6178 Mitch Owen Rd.
P.O. Box 700
Manotick, ON
Canada K4M 1A6
613-822-6800
www.wood-source.com
Wood supply

ADJUSTABLE CLAMP COMPANY
404 N. Armour St.
Chicago, IL 60622
312-666-0640
www.adjustableclamp.com
Clamps and woodworking tools

B&Q
B&Q Head Office
Portswood House
1 Hampshire Corporate Park
Chandlers Ford
Eastleigh
Hampshire SO53 3YX
0845 609 6688
www.diy.com
Woodworking tools, supplies and hardware

CONSTANTINE'S WOOD CENTER OF FLORIDA
1040 E. Oakland Park Blvd.
Fort Lauderdale, FL 33334
800-443-9667
www.constantines.com
Tools, woods, veneers, hardware

FRANK PAXTON LUMBER COMPANY
5701 W. 66th St.
Chicago, IL 60638
800-323-2203
www.paxtonwood.com
Wood, hardware, tools, books

THE HOME DEPOT
2455 Paces Ferry Rd.
Atlanta, GA 30339
800-553-3199 (U.S.)
800-668-0525 (Canada)
www.homedepot.com
Woodworking tools, supplies and hardware

LEE VALLEY TOOLS LTD.
P.O. Box 1780
Ogdensburg, NY 13669-6780
800-871-8158 (U.S.)
800-267-8767 (Canada)
www.leevalley.com
Woodworking tools and hardware

LOWE'S HOME IMPROVEMENT WAREHOUSE
P.O. Box 1111
North Wilkesboro, NC 28656
800-445-6937
www.lowes.com
Woodworking tools, supplies and hardware

ROCKLER WOODWORKING AND HARDWARE
4365 Willow Dr.
Medina, MN 55340
800-279-4441
www.rockler.com
Woodworking tools, hardware and books

ROO PRODUCTS INC.
PO Box 299
Woodburn, OR 97071
877-766-4583
www.rooglue.com
Purveyors of fine adhesives

TOOL TREND LTD.
140 Snow Blvd.
Thornhill, ON
Canada L4K 4L1
416-663-8665
Woodworking tools and hardware

TREND MACHINERY & CUTTING TOOLS LTD.
Odhams Trading Estate
St. Albans Road
Watford
Hertfordshire, U.K.
WD24 7TR
01923 224657
www.trendmachinery.co.uk
Woodworking tools and hardware

VAUGHAN & BUSHNELL MFG. CO.
11414 Maple Ave.
Hebron, IL 60034
815-648-2446
www.vaughanmfg.com
Hammers and other tools

WOODCRAFT
406 Airport Industrial Park Rd.
P.O. Box 1686
Parkersburg, WV 26104
800-535-4482
www.woodcraft.com
Woodworking hardware

WOODWORKER'S HARDWARE
P.O. Box 180
Sauk Rapids, MN 56379-0180
800-383-0130
www.wwhardware.com
Woodworking hardware

WOODWORKER'S SUPPLY
1108 North Glenn Rd.
Casper, WY 82601
800-645-9292
http://woodworker.com
Woodworking tools and accessoried, finishing supplies, books and plans

index

More great titles from Popular Woodworking!

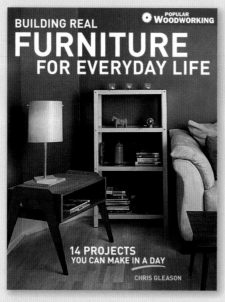
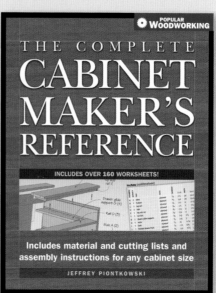
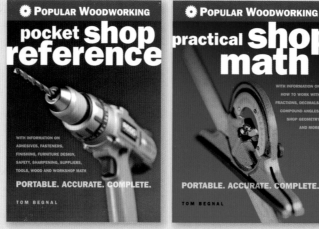